The Duffs
AND THE
MacKinnons

NEIGHBORS FOR GENERATIONS

The Duffs
AND THE
MacKinnons

NEIGHBORS FOR GENERATIONS

William H. Duff

Genealogy House
Amherst, Massachusetts

First published 2019 by Genealogy House
Publishers of Family History and Genealogy, a division of White River Press LLC,
PO Box 3561, Amherst, MA 01004 • www.genealogyhouse.net

ISBN: 978-1-887043-44-1

Book Design by Lufkin Graphic Designs, Norwich, Vermont
www.lufkingraphics.com

Library of Congress Cataloging-in-Publication Data

Names: Duff, William H., 1949- author.
Title: The Duffs and the MacKinnons : neighbors for generations / William H.
   Duff.
Description: Amherst, Massachusetts : Genealogy House Publishers, 2018. |
   Includes bibliographical references. | Audience: "The story and genealogy
   of two immigrant next-door neighbors in Boston whose children married in
   1937. Both families came to Boston via the Canadian Maritimes: the Duffs
   came from Ireland to Newfoundland, while the MacKinnons came from Scotland
   to Nova Scotia."--Provided by publisher.
Identifiers: LCCN 2018048032 | ISBN 9781887043441 (hardcover : alk. paper)
Subjects: LCSH: Boston (Mass.)--Genealogy. | Duff family. | McKinnon family.
Classification: LCC F73.25 D84 2018 | DDC 929.20973--dc23
LC record available at https://lccn.loc.gov/2018048032

DEDICATION

I wish to dedicate this book to my wife Leigh who has been my motivator, best friend, and soul mate for over 50 years. Without her endless enthusiasm and unyielding support, this book would never have become a reality.

The sacrifice our ancestors gave yesterday gave us today and our tomorrow.

— *Stephen Robert Kuta*

When our hearts turn to our ancestors, something changes inside us. We feel part of something greater than ourselves.

— *Russell M. Nelson*

Why waste your money looking up your family tree? Just go into politics and your opponents will do it for you.

— *Mark Twain*

CONTENTS

DESCENDANT CHART
FOR JOHN MACKINNON

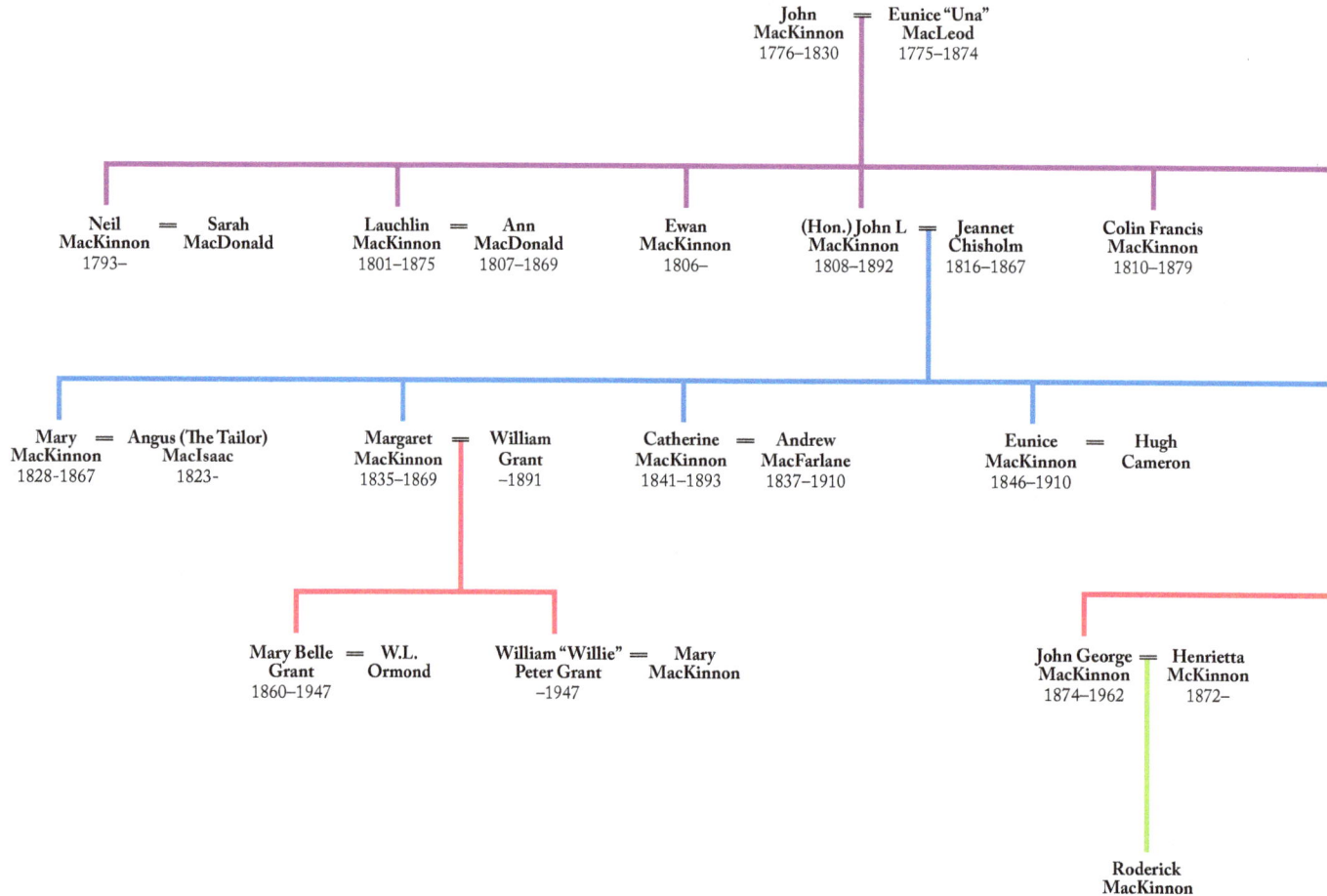

John MacKinnon 1776–1830 = **Eunice "Una" MacLeod** 1775–1874

- **Neil MacKinnon** 1793– = **Sarah MacDonald**
- **Lauchlin MacKinnon** 1801–1875 = **Ann MacDonald** 1807–1869
- **Ewan MacKinnon** 1806–
- **(Hon.) John L MacKinnon** 1808–1892 = **Jeannet Chisholm** 1816–1867
- **Colin Francis MacKinnon** 1810–1879

- **Mary MacKinnon** 1828-1867 = **Angus (The Tailor) MacIsaac** 1823–
- **Margaret MacKinnon** 1835–1869 = **William Grant** –1891
- **Catherine MacKinnon** 1841–1893 = **Andrew MacFarlane** 1837–1910
- **Eunice MacKinnon** 1846–1910 = **Hugh Cameron**

- **Mary Belle Grant** 1860–1947 = **W.L. Ormond**
- **William "Willie" Peter Grant** –1947 = **Mary MacKinnon**

- **John George MacKinnon** 1874–1962 = **Henrietta McKinnon** 1872–

- **Roderick MacKinnon**

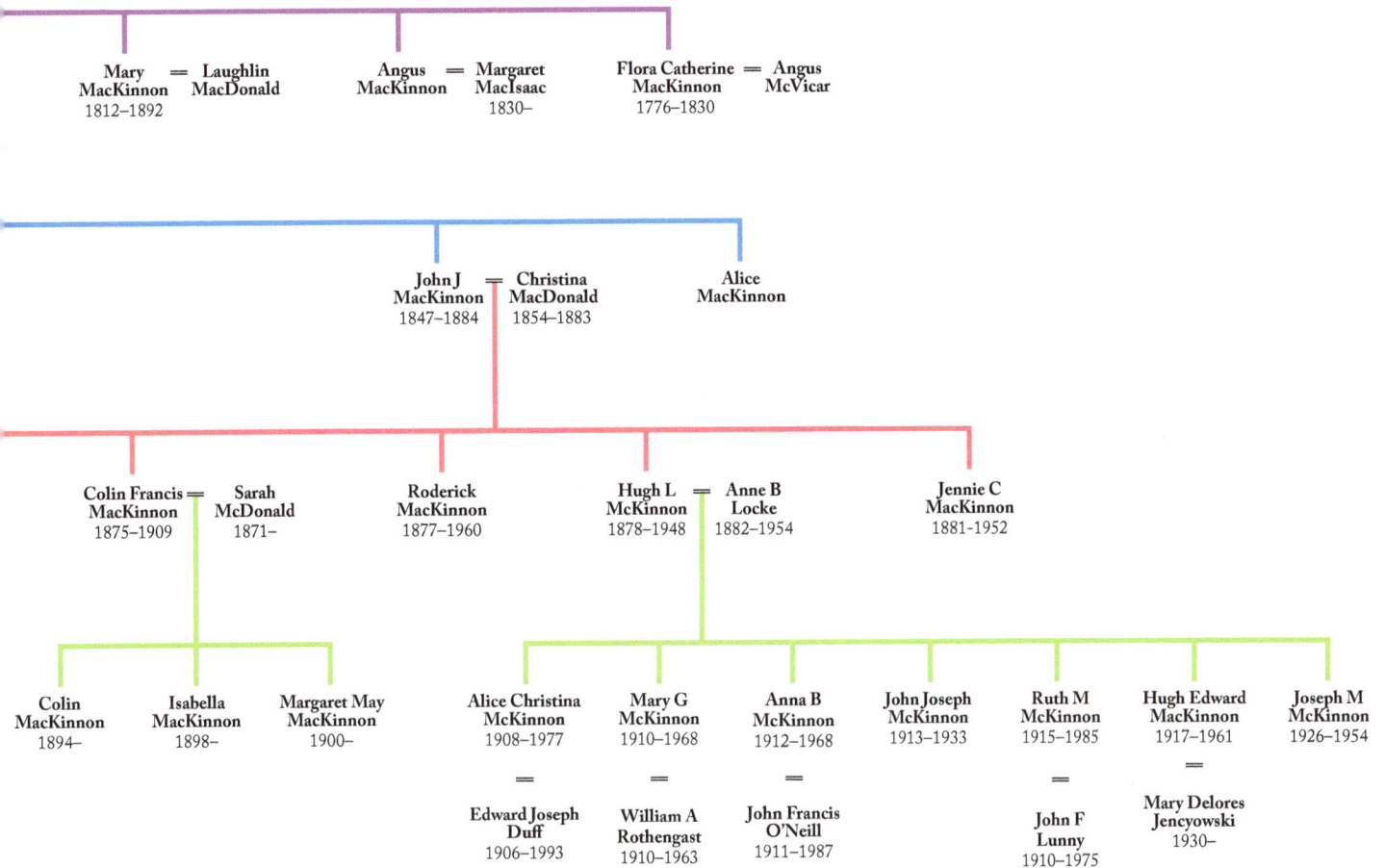

Mary
MacKinnon
1812–1892
= Laughlin
MacDonald

Angus
MacKinnon
= Margaret
MacIsaac
1830–

Flora Catherine
MacKinnon
1776–1830
= Angus
McVicar

John J
MacKinnon
1847–1884
= Christina
MacDonald
1854–1883

Alice
MacKinnon

Colin Francis
MacKinnon
1875–1909
= Sarah
McDonald
1871–

Roderick
MacKinnon
1877–1960

Hugh L
McKinnon
1878–1948
= Anne B
Locke
1882–1954

Jennie C
MacKinnon
1881-1952

Colin
MacKinnon
1894–

Isabella
MacKinnon
1898–

Margaret May
MacKinnon
1900–

Alice Christina
McKinnon
1908–1977
=
Edward Joseph
Duff
1906–1993

Mary G
McKinnon
1910–1968
=
William A
Rothengast
1910–1963

Anna B
McKinnon
1912–1968
=
John Francis
O'Neill
1911–1987

John Joseph
McKinnon
1913–1933

Ruth M
McKinnon
1915–1985
=
John F
Lunny
1910–1975

Hugh Edward
MacKinnon
1917–1961
=
Mary Delores
Jencyowski
1930–

Joseph M
McKinnon
1926–1954

DESCENDANT CHART
FOR ARTHUR DUFF / DUFFE

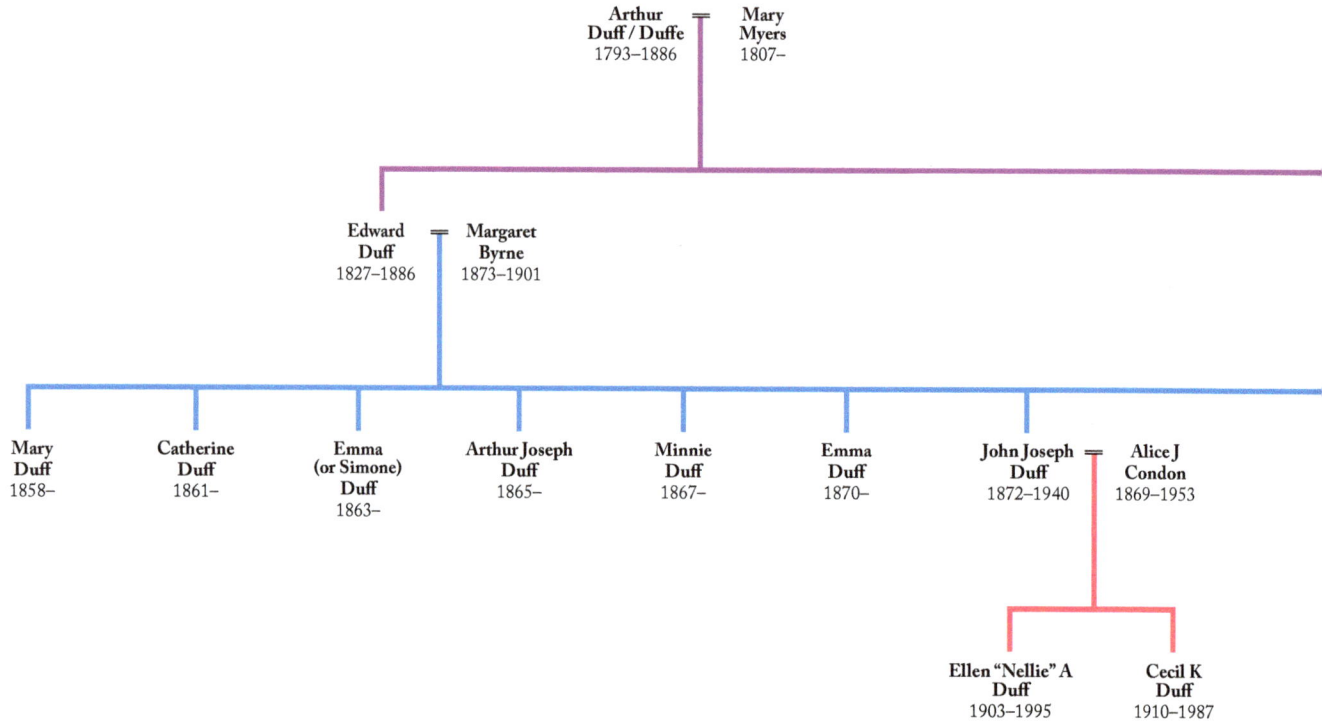

Arthur Duff / Duffe
1793–1886
=
Mary Myers
1807–

Edward Duff
1827–1886
=
Margaret Byrne
1873–1901

Mary Duff
1858–

Catherine Duff
1861–

Emma (or Simone) Duff
1863–

Arthur Joseph Duff
1865–

Minnie Duff
1867–

Emma Duff
1870–

John Joseph Duff
1872–1940
=
Alice J Condon
1869–1953

Ellen "Nellie" A Duff
1903–1995

Cecil K Duff
1910–1987

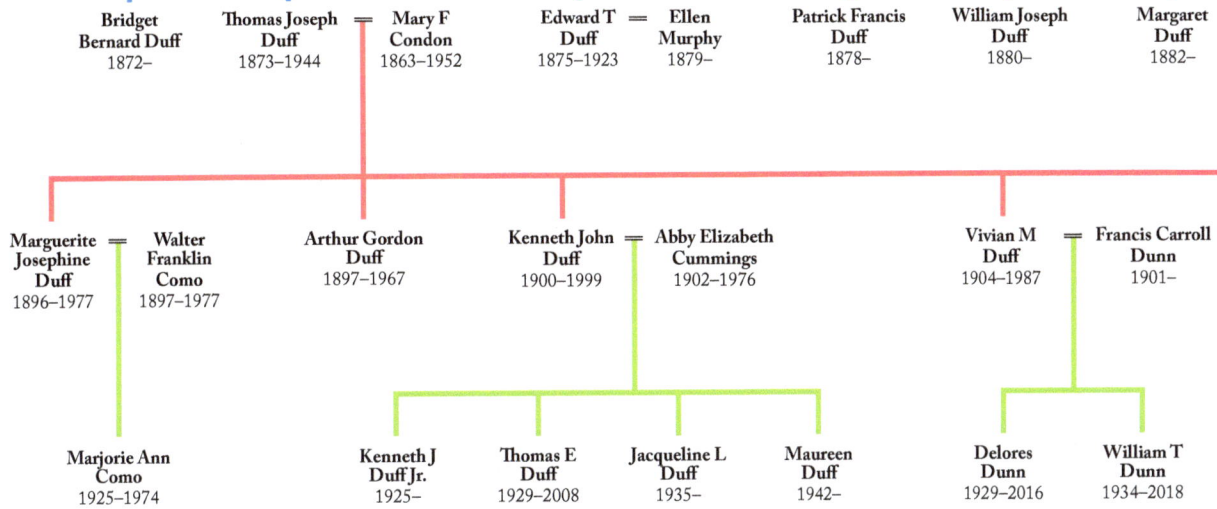

Bridget Bernard Duff 1872–

Thomas Joseph Duff 1873–1944 = **Mary F Condon** 1863–1952

Edward T Duff 1875–1923 = **Ellen Murphy** 1879–

Patrick Francis Duff 1878–

William Joseph Duff 1880–

Margaret Duff 1882–

Marguerite Josephine Duff 1896–1977 = **Walter Franklin Como** 1897–1977

Arthur Gordon Duff 1897–1967

Kenneth John Duff 1900–1999 = **Abby Elizabeth Cummings** 1902–1976

Vivian M Duff 1904–1987 = **Francis Carroll Dunn** 1901–

Marjorie Ann Como 1925–1974

Kenneth J Duff Jr. 1925–

Thomas E Duff 1929–2008

Jacqueline L Duff 1935–

Maureen Duff 1942–

Delores Dunn 1929–2016

William T Dunn 1934–2018

E   THE DUFFS AND THE MacKINNONS

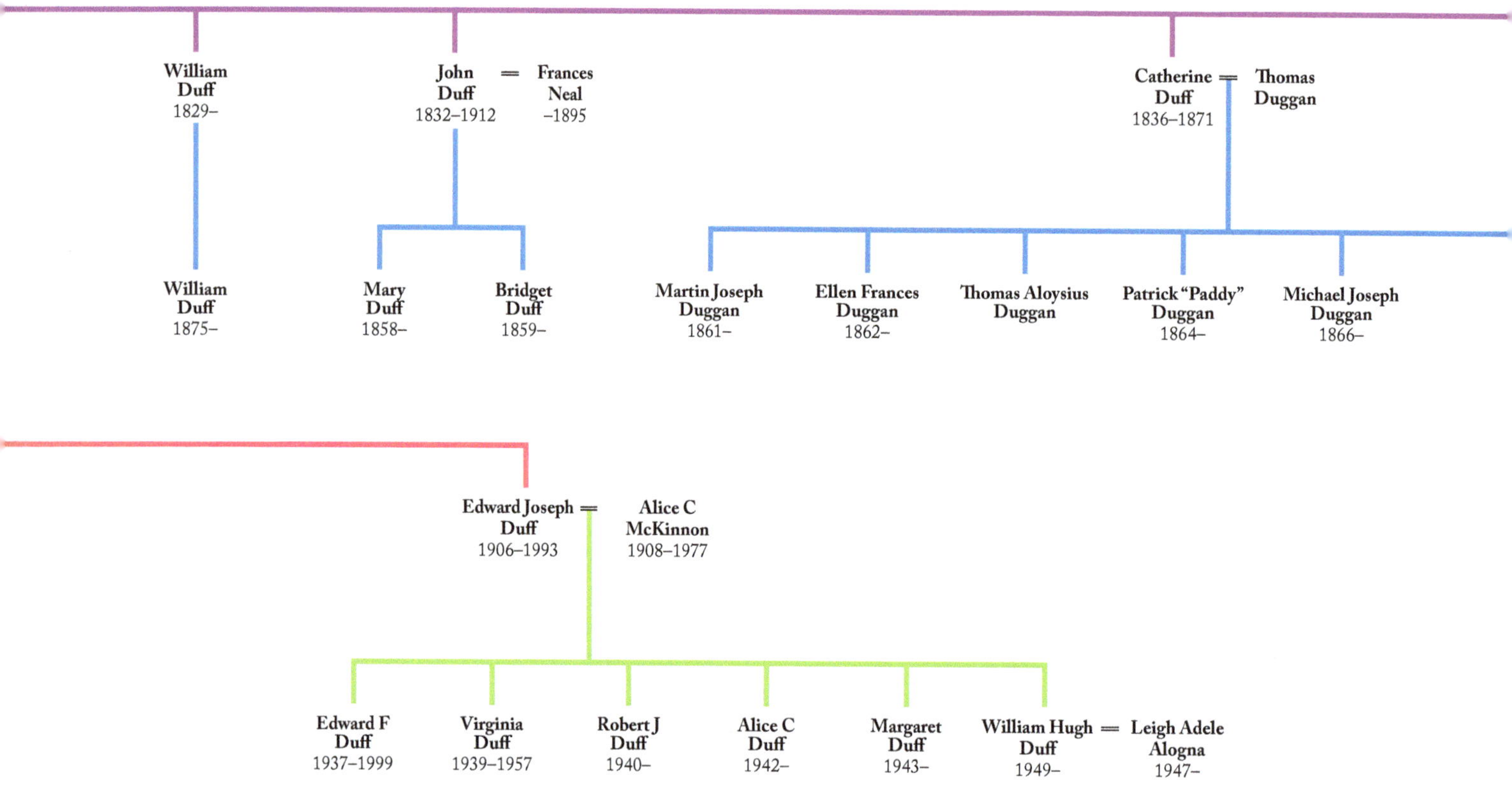

William
Duff
1829–

John
Duff = Frances
1832–1912   Neal
–1895

Catherine = Thomas
Duff   Duggan
1836–1871

William
Duff
1875–

Mary
Duff
1858–

Bridget
Duff
1859–

Martin Joseph
Duggan
1861–

Ellen Frances
Duggan
1862–

Thomas Aloysius
Duggan

Patrick "Paddy"
Duggan
1864–

Michael Joseph
Duggan
1866–

Edward Joseph = Alice C
Duff   McKinnon
1906–1993   1908–1977

Edward F
Duff
1937–1999

Virginia
Duff
1939–1957

Robert J
Duff
1940–

Alice C
Duff
1942–

Margaret
Duff
1943–

William Hugh = Leigh Adele
Duff   Alogna
1949–   1947–

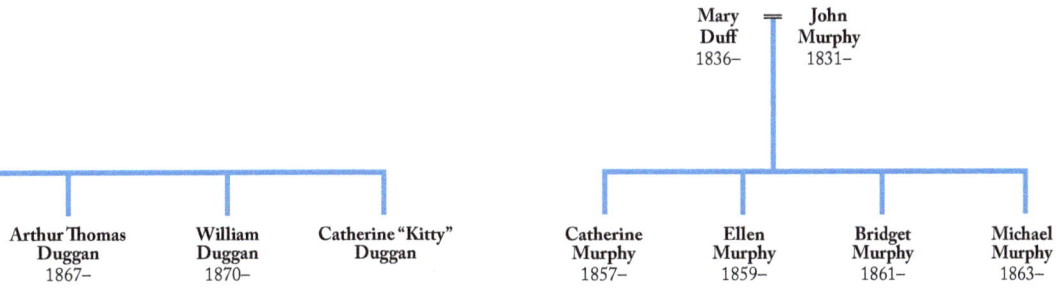

Mary
Duff
1836–
=
John
Murphy
1831–

**Arthur Thomas
Duggan**
1867–

**William
Duggan**
1870–

**Catherine "Kitty"
Duggan**

**Catherine
Murphy**
1857–

**Ellen
Murphy**
1859–

**Bridget
Murphy**
1861–

**Michael
Murphy**
1863–

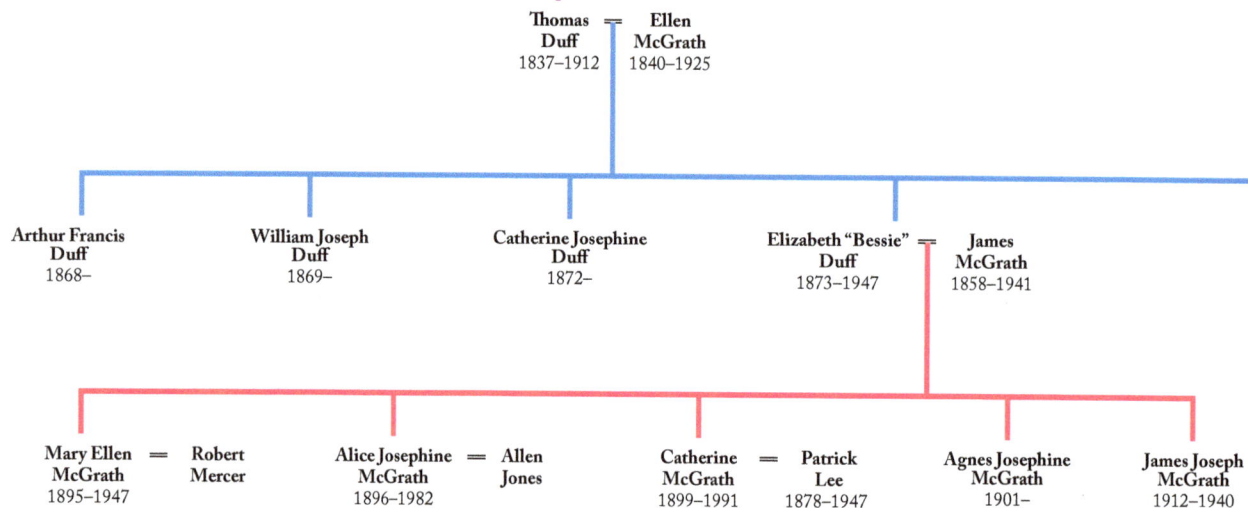

Thomas Duff 1837–1912 = Ellen McGrath 1840–1925

Arthur Francis Duff 1868–

William Joseph Duff 1869–

Catherine Josephine Duff 1872–

Elizabeth "Bessie" Duff 1873–1947 = James McGrath 1858–1941

Mary Ellen McGrath 1895–1947 = Robert Mercer

Alice Josephine McGrath 1896–1982 = Allen Jones

Catherine McGrath 1899–1991 = Patrick Lee 1878–1947

Agnes Josephine McGrath 1901–

James Joseph McGrath 1912–1940

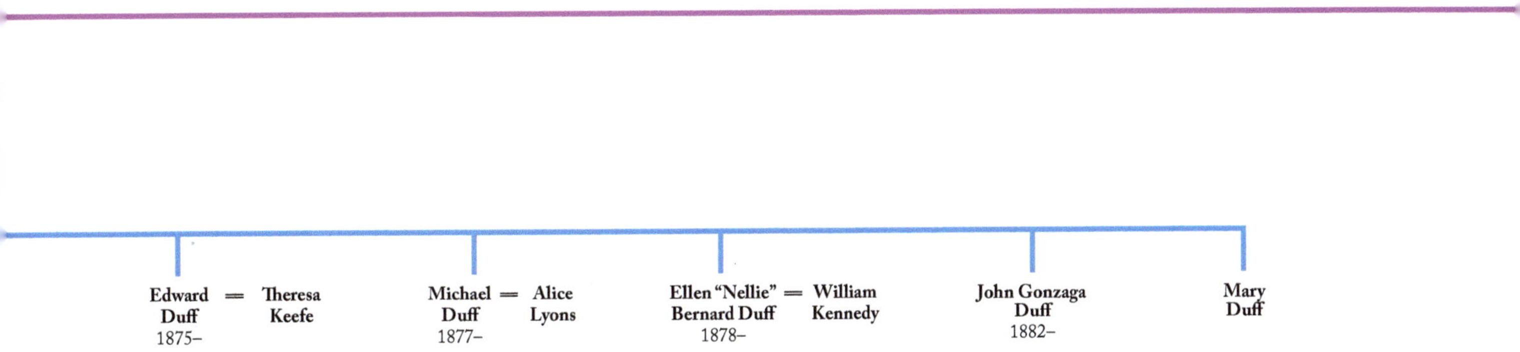

Edward
Duff
1875–
= Theresa
Keefe

Michael
Duff
1877–
= Alice
Lyons

Ellen "Nellie"
Bernard Duff
1878–
= William
Kennedy

John Gonzaga
Duff
1882–

Mary
Duff

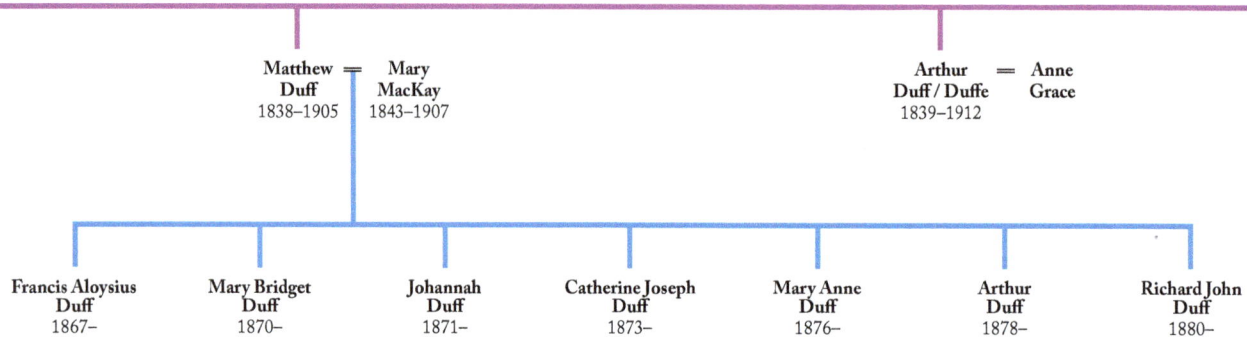

Matthew Duff 1838–1905 = Mary MacKay 1843–1907

Arthur Duff / Duffe 1839–1912 = Anne Grace

Francis Aloysius Duff 1867–

Mary Bridget Duff 1870–

Johannah Duff 1871–

Catherine Joseph Duff 1873–

Mary Anne Duff 1876–

Arthur Duff 1878–

Richard John Duff 1880–

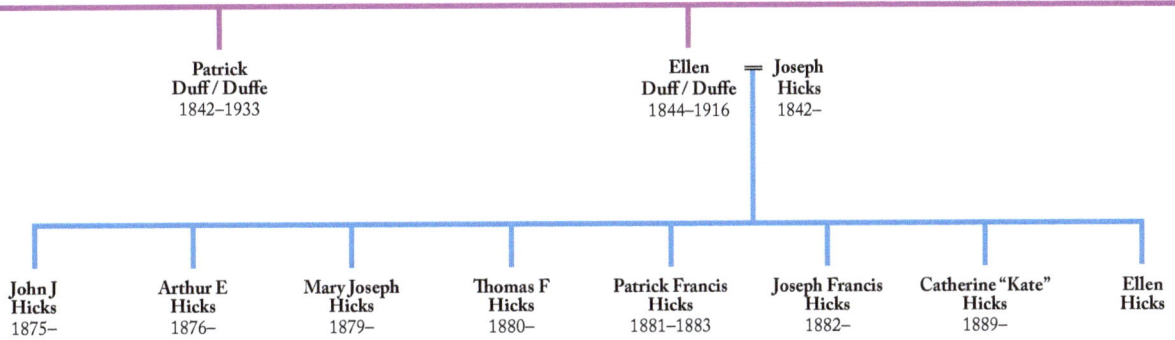

**Patrick
Duff / Duffe**
1842–1933

**Ellen
Duff / Duffe**
1844–1916

**Joseph
Hicks**
1842–

**John J
Hicks**
1875–

**Arthur E
Hicks**
1876–

**Mary Joseph
Hicks**
1879–

**Thomas F
Hicks**
1880–

**Patrick Francis
Hicks**
1881–1883

**Joseph Francis
Hicks**
1882–

**Catherine "Kate"
Hicks**
1889–

**Ellen
Hicks**

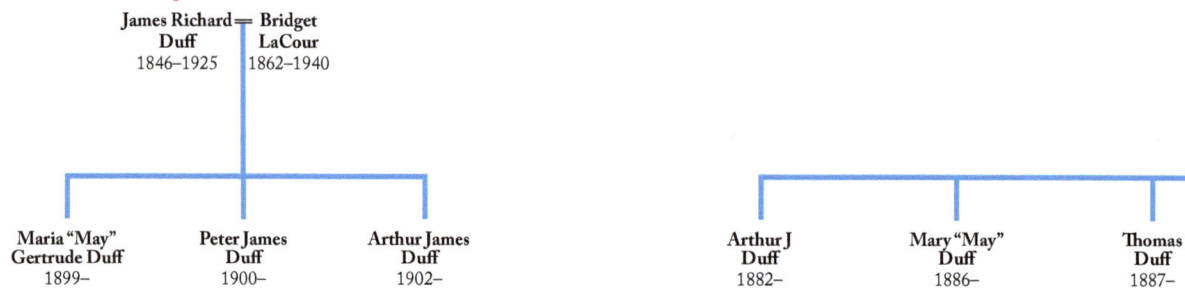

James Richard ═ Bridget
Duff   LaCour
1846–1925   1862–1940

Maria "May"   Peter James   Arthur James
Gertrude Duff   Duff   Duff
1899–   1900–   1902–

Arthur J   Mary "May"   Thomas
Duff   Duff   Duff
1882–   1886–   1887–

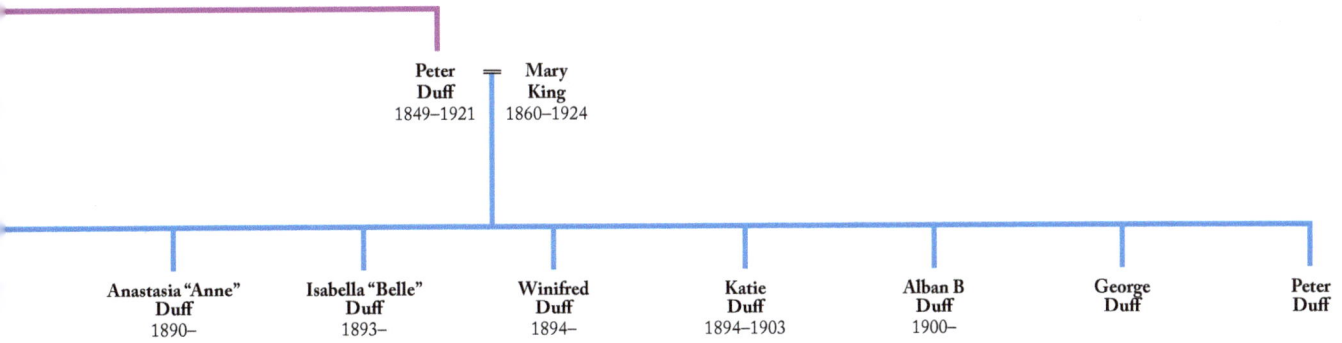

Peter
Duff
1849–1921

Mary
King
1860–1924

Anastasia "Anne"
Duff
1890–

Isabella "Belle"
Duff
1893–

Winifred
Duff
1894–

Katie
Duff
1894–1903

Alban B
Duff
1900–

George
Duff

Peter
Duff

PREFACE

As noted by the cover's image, the title and theme of this book includes the word "Neighbors." Although the Duffs and the MacKinnons emigrated from different European countries, namely Ireland and Scotland, both are geographically neighbors. When the respective families immigrated to the New World toward the end of the eighteenth century, they settled in two Canadian Maritime Provinces—Newfoundland and Nova Scotia—both of which are neighbors. And when my respective grandparents sought a better life in the States at the end of the nineteenth century, they bought adjacent homes in the same city, in the same neighborhood, on the same street. They were neighbors. So, after residing in their respective homes for some twenty years, how ironic it was that my father courted and married the girl next door.

Despite the many hours of research, writing, and travel, this was an enjoyable project. It was interesting work, and it needed to be done. With so much commercial advertising on family history sites and DNA testing today, there has been a growing interest among people to learn where they came from. To those who have committed themselves to the project of family history, I commend their enthusiasm and initiative because it's not an easy task. Sometimes the decision to pursue this goal came either out of curiosity or guilt. For me it was a little bit of both.

The idea to discover my family origin began several years ago in Miami when I attended an annual luncheon for retired FBI Agents. I was sitting with a small group of new friends after the meal when one gentleman raised the topic of genealogy. He described the success he'd had in tracing his family back through several generations in the Dakotas and ultimately to Scandinavia. A second gentleman in the group piped in to describe the luck he'd had with the vast genealogy database maintained by the Church of Latter Day Saints in Utah. He had a German surname and had been able to trace his "roots" through several generations in the Midwest back to Western Europe. He had no problem reciting the names and occupations of his most notable ancestors going back to the sixteenth century. He had even used DNA testing. Both of these gents had spent a fair amount of time over the past few years dedicated to this project. How impressive!

At that point, I wish they had dropped the subject, as I knew what would happen next: they asked if I knew my genealogy. I tried to gloss over the question, because I knew I didn't have a clue. It's not as if when I was growing up my family sat around the kitchen table and listened to Dad relating stories about his ancestors. It just didn't happen. My father was a longshoreman on the Boston waterfront and could be described as a *no BS* type of guy. Besides, I was the youngest of six by a long shot (six years younger than my older sister), and stories of my grandparents or previous generations rarely trickled down. At mealtime, my father was more concerned with ensuring that the after-supper chores (e.g., dishes and trash) were done quickly and without hesitation. Raising some other topic was not advisable.

After a moment or two of hesitation (a pregnant pause, if you will), I told my new friends that learning about our ancestors just hadn't been a priority in my family. However, I did know that my mother's family was from Nova Scotia, and Dad's family . . . well . . . I was not so sure about them. In terms of nationality, I thought (guessing now!) that Mom was Scottish and English, and Dad was most likely the same. That was essentially it! The Swede and the German at the table didn't have to say a word: their expressions said it all. I felt like putting on the proverbial "dunce cap" after being told to stand in the corner and face the wall until I could think of something more intelligent to say. It's interesting to note what a little humiliation flavored with embarrassment will do to motivate.

As a sidelight, I had been to Scotland in the late 1990s in connection with a trip to London, and I had actually found a small town in the northeast region known as Duff Town. Besides its nineteenth-century history of housing soldiers returning from the Napoleonic Wars, it is also situated remarkably close to the single malt Scotch distilleries of Glenfiddich and Balvenie, both of which are near and dear to my heart. I learned then that a certain "Duff House"—a grand mansion on an impressive estate—stands in nearby Banff. Now part of the National

Galleries of Scotland, this stately house was designed by William Adam in 1735 and was widely thought to be one of the world's finest Georgian houses. It was built for none other than "William Duff" who became the Earl of Fife in 1759. Since that visit to Scotland, I have even kept a framed image of the Duff House in my home in Connecticut. This had to be where it all had started, or so I wanted to believe. But even if the royal bloodline was a bit of a stretch, there was no doubt in my mind that my Duff ancestors once roamed the Scottish Highlands.

Despite that the experience at the luncheon might have been the catalyst, it took me a couple of years to finally make finding my roots a priority and actually do something about it. It was not as if there weren't stories to be told. My brothers had a ton of them. But they mostly focused on my aunts and uncles as well as my McKinnon grandparents, all of whom had grown up in Neponset, in the southeast corner of Dorchester, in Boston. My (McKinnon) cousins, especially the O'Neills and the Lunnys, were also quite knowledgeable, but again, they didn't know much back beyond a few generations, and certainly nothing that would help pull all the information together. I knew that my cousin Jack O'Neill and his wife, Barbara, had not only visited Nova Scotia, but also had traveled to the Isle of Eigg in Scotland to trace the family on that side of the Atlantic. But being the youngest of the family and having left the Boston area at age 21 to go into the service, I hadn't had much exposure to any details that might be available.

If I knew little about my mother's family, I knew even less about the Duffs. In fact, to say I knew somewhere between a "lot less" and nothing at all would be appropriate. So, a few years ago, I decided to gather some preliminary information on my dad's parents. Finding out where they were buried appeared to be an easy start. So I thought. When I learned that none of my siblings knew, I started cold calling the cemeteries in Boston. I had no idea how many cemeteries there are in the Boston area. Luckily my grandparents were practicing Catholics, so I soon narrowed the search to St. Joseph's in West Roxbury, MA.

Finding the headstone (if there is one) is like Genealogy 101. It's a must and a great starting point as it provides the full name of the deceased, the birth and death dates, and with whom they are buried. In addition, by checking with the cemetery office, anyone can determine who had paid for the lot, or at least had arranged for the burial. In this case, my grandfather Thomas J. Duff (d. 1944) was buried with my grandmother Mary F. Duff (d. 1952), and my uncle Arthur G. Duff (d. 1967).

Since I was born in 1949, I had no recollection of having met either my Duff grandmother or my uncle Arthur, who had moved to California years before I was born and had stayed there his entire life.

Headstone of Thomas and Mary Duff, St. Joseph's Cemetery, W. Roxbury, MA.

*Front and back of
the McKinnon/Duff
headstone in Milton
Cemetery, Milton, MA.*

This information was in sharp contrast to what I knew about my mother's family, the McKinnons. My parents, my McKinnon grandparents, my brother Ed, sister Ginny, some uncles, etc. are all buried in the same plot at Milton Cemetery within walking distance from where we grew up. I had full names, pertinent dates, the whole "enchilada"—one-stop shopping, if you will.

Because I seemed to know more about the McKinnons, I thought I should tackle that side first. I decided to begin by gathering whatever information was available online. I found a variety of search engines that offered bits and pieces, but for the most part, the fees were exorbitant, and they did not seem designed specifically for genealogical research. Then, after seeing numerous ads for Ancestry.com, I decided to give it a try. I have not been disappointed.

My cousins Jack O'Neill and Jim Lunny had been to Nova Scotia several times and my brother Bob at least once. If I was going to take this project (at least somewhat) seriously, I knew that I, too, should make the trip. So, my wife, Leigh, and I decided to fly up to Halifax in the summer of 2013 and rent a car for the better part of two weeks. I wanted to see firsthand where the McKinnon clan had originated, settled, and died. It turned out to be a great trip as we parlayed it with visits to the provinces of New Brunswick and Prince Edward Island.

When we arrived at the Antigonish Heritage Museum, we were greeted by the proprietor, Jocelyn, a lovely woman who provided literally a treasure trove of information.

We had allocated four or five days to spend doing research at various locations including the town hall, church, library, cemetery, etc. But as it turned out, students at St. Francis Xavier University (located in Antigonish) who work part time at the museum for academic

Antigonish Town Hall.

Antigonish restaurant.

credit assist in the automation of hard copy genealogical records. To my surprise, Jocelyn was able to generate a complete family tree listing of the descendants of (pioneer) John MacKinnon from the late 1700s all the way to my mother's generation. This listing included the names of all family tree members along with their places and dates of births, marriages, and deaths. Occupations were also included as they'd been available. This was the closest I had come to hitting the lottery. In less than one hour, I had just saved myself most likely four or five days of work.

The Antigonish Heritage Museum, Antigonish, Nova Scotia, Canada.

The old MacKinnon House, built in 1815,
in Williams Point, Antigonish.

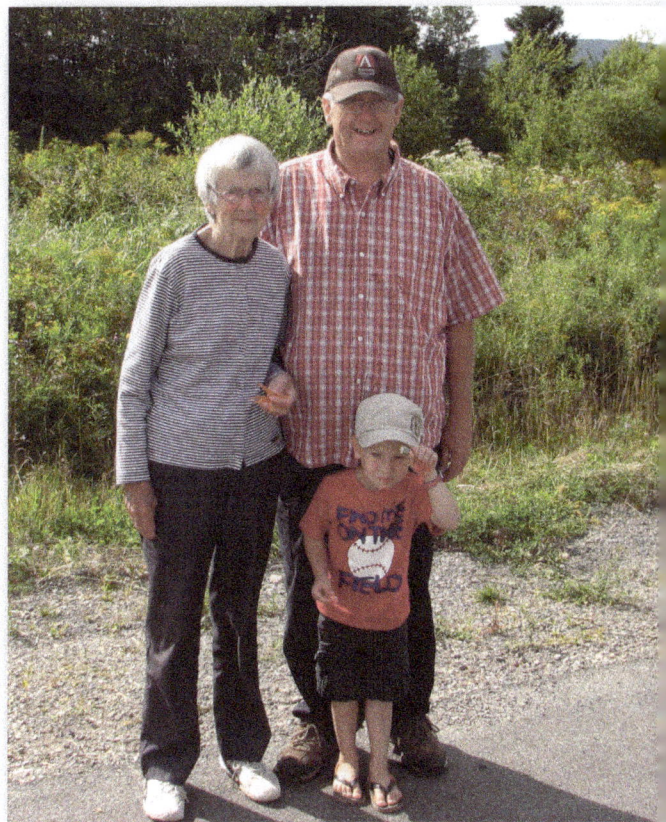

Kitty MacFarlane, her son, and grandson

A second treat we experienced in Antigonish was when we visited the old MacKinnon homestead, which is in a section of town known as Williams Point. Jocelyn put us in touch with (Mrs.) Kitty MacFarlane who had occupied the house since 1961. She was in her nineties then and couldn't have been more hospitable. The house, which was built in 1815, was the childhood home of my grandfather Hugh L. McKinnon, his father, John J. MacKinnon, and John's father, Honorable John

MacKinnon. I will always be grateful to Kitty for taking the time to share her recollections of the old homestead for most of the last 100 years!

Edward Joseph Duff's birth certificate.

After spending a few days in Antigonish, I learned that if there is one family that has had a profound impact on the town, it is the MacKinnons, primarily due to the accomplishments of my grandfather's great-uncle Bishop Colin MacKinnon. Bishop MacKinnon is credited with founding the prestigious St. Andrew's Boys School in Antigonish in 1838, and St. Francis Xavier University, which began as a seminary in 1853 and is rated as one of the top five universities in Canada today. A few years later, Bishop MacKinnon announced his vision for St. Ninian's Cathedral in Antigonish, then he followed it through from planning to completion.

After making a few other contacts in the town, we left with the satisfaction of knowing we had a pretty good grasp of the MacKinnon family, at least to the point of their emigration from Scotland in the late eighteenth century.

But if the trip to Nova Scotia was not the challenge I had envisioned, the following year's trip to Newfoundland (NL) more than made up for the shortfall. Other than the inscriptions on the Duff gravestone at St. Joseph's Cemetery, the only information I had was a copy of my father's birth certificate that listed my grandparents' place of birth as St. John's, Newfoundland (NL), and some sketchy details from Ancestry. com. Presuming that a good starting point would be St. John's, Leigh and I spent four days there, visiting various offices and libraries that cater to genealogical research.

In addition to canvassing the Canadian internet sites that were recommended, we searched records at the Provincial Archives of Newfoundland and Labrador (known as the "Rooms"), which is a state-of-the-art facility opened in 2005. We spent another day at the Genealogy Center at Memorial University of Newfoundland, also in St. John's. In addition, the archivist at the Basilica of St. John the Baptist—the repository of baptismal, marriage, and death records for the Archdiocese of St. John's—searched more records. All in all, the results were terribly disappointing, if not disheartening. There were simply no records of my grandparents. It was almost as if I had the wrong Canadian province, despite the fact that staff members were sympathetic and offered a variety of explanations. Maybe I had the wrong city. Though "NL" was clearly noted on the birth certificate, could it have been the city of St. John in New Brunswick? Maybe the records were under a derivative name such as MacDuff or Duffin. Or perhaps our family records had been destroyed in one of the three major fires that devastated St. John's in the nineteenth century, the worst in 1892 which destroyed almost a third of the city. Regardless of the reason, the records were simply not to be found.

One of the archivists suggested that we check the Duff name in E.R. Seary's book, *Family Names of the Island of Newfoundland*, which lists the presence of a particular surname in any town or region of NL. It was very general in nature and certainly a long shot at best. Nonetheless, we made a mental note of the names of some of the small towns, but we didn't hold much optimism. After all, most of NL and Labrador are still the wild frontier. Other than St. John's, all the towns are small!

But on the fifth day, we finally had some luck. We left St. John's for Trinity, an historic fishing village, some 150 miles west of the capital for general sightseeing. Searching for fuel, we exited the Trans-Canadian highway just outside of St. John's at a small town called Holyrood, one of many listed in the Seary book. When asked about any Duff families in the area, a teenage girl at the gas station checkout said, "Nope," but added that there was a Duff Road up the highway apiece, "but no Duffs live there." She also suggested we stop by an old Catholic cemetery a few miles away. Duff Road was there but offered no clues. Similarly, we found several Duff stones in the old cemetery, illustrating that "a Duff" family had, in fact, lived in this region for over a century. But there was no indication that *this* Duff family was in any way related to *my* Duff family.

Still disappointed, we stopped for lunch at The Station Diner in Holyrood, site of the old railroad station. We decided that the second half of our journey would be entirely focused on sightseeing and visiting historical points of interest. As the waitress handed me the check, I couldn't help but ask if there was anyone in Holyrood who might be

Holyrood sign.

Holy Cross Cemetery.

knowledgeable of the town's history, or better still, someone who could assist in tracing one's family. She said that no one came to mind, but she suggested I might put in a call to Joe Byrne who was apparently well known in the town and had an office in the library just up the street. A local historian, if you will, Joe was a former teacher and loved to chat with tourists and others who were trying to trace their family roots.

After lunch, we continued as planned on a sightseeing trip to the historic fishing village of Trinity, some three hours northwest of St. John's. Founded by the Portuguese in 1501, Trinity is a charming, historical fishing village with beautifully preserved eighteenth-century buildings à la Williamsburg-style. In its heyday, it was the merchant center for the export of cod and of seal pelts, and for whale oil produced in Newfoundland. One thing present day Trinity does not enjoy, however, is adequate cell phone reception.

Nonetheless, over the next few days and after numerous dropped calls, we made arrangements to meet Joe Byrne on our way back to St. John's. The meeting finally took place in a small corner office of the town library, a place Joe calls his second home. He's a middle-aged man with a broad smile, firm handshake, and thick accent. I soon learned that there were two components to Joe's accent: first and foremost is the Newfoundland twang that becomes more evident the farther you venture from St. John's; second, we were in what was historically an Irish settlement, and Joe's predominant Irish brogue was no exception.

I proceeded to explain that after spending four days in St. John's searching for records, I had essentially given up hope. After asking a

The author (me!) with dried cod in Trinity.

few questions about my grandparents, Joe muttered an "Um" or two and began to pull very old files from a very old metal filing cabinet. He quickly put on his reading glasses (tip of the nose, of course) as if he had found something of interest. I gave my wife my tried and true "this is a total waste of time" glance, which she is accustomed to. Nevertheless, I then continued to watch Joe as he meticulously unfolded a multi-page, hand-written, penciled chart, which, judging by its shade of yellow, had been Scotch-taped together many years before and hadn't seen the light of day for many years beyond that. Certainly, it offered no semblance to the automated filing systems we had witnessed in St. John's.

Near Trinity Bay.

Joe's only utterance at that point was: "Where you from again?" When I reminded him for the third time that my grandfather had migrated to the Boston area, he exclaimed, "Oh ya, you're the Boston Duffs!" Then he added with an impish smile, "What took you so long? I've been waiting for you folks a long time."

When we asked what he meant, Joe said his great-grandfather's sister was Margaret Byrne who was my great-grandmother, thus making us distant cousins! He then confirmed the connection by tracing his hand-written family tree with a pencil and literally "connecting the dots" (to my amazement) to my great-grandparents. Simply put, my great-grandmother was the sister of Joe's great-grandfather Peter. Needless to say, we were ecstatic, if not speechless! What a remarkable find by pure happenstance after all this time, and just when we were ready to head home empty-handed.

Apparently, Joe could tell by our expressions that we were delighted with the news. I had finally found where my grandfather lived before immigrating to the States in the late 1800s and where his father (my great grandfather) had grown up. There was so much still to learn, but at least now I had a starting point. Then, almost as if on cue, when we got up to leave, Joe said he wanted to set the record straight. In his thick Irish brogue, he said in no uncertain terms, "You're no more Scottish than I am. You're from Wexford, Ireland, and be proud of it!" That put a smile on everyone's face.

Joe then took us to lunch at an old home that had been converted to a restaurant. It was located across the street from the diner near the railroad tracks where we had lunched a few days earlier. He then

Joe Byrne and me in front of Margaret Byrne's old home.

pointed out the home had been where my great-grandmother Margaret Byrne had lived.

For several days, we spent hours perusing old records and emails Joe had accumulated that pertained to the Duff family. He explained that my grandfather had grown up in an area of Holyrood known as "Duffs" and not in St. John's as I'd been led to believe. He also connected the dots between my great-grandparents and their extended families. And he took us down to "Duff's Road" and pointed out where my ancestors had lived many years before.

Joe also put us in touch with other cousins in Newfoundland, including Alice Finn and her husband, Mike, who live in St. John's. Alice is a wonderful person and a treasure of family information. In fact, she volunteers at the Genealogical Center at the Provincial Archives in St. John's.

Alice Finn with me in 2016.

Alice Finn, her husband, Mike, and Leigh.

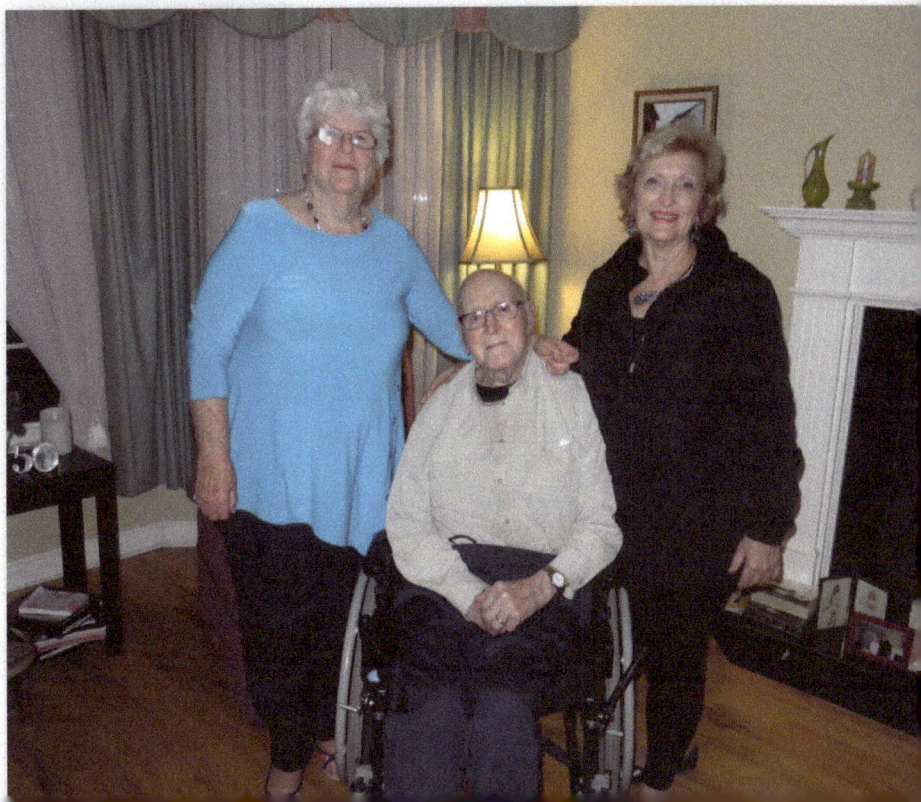

Duff's Road.

Needless to say, our trip had been more than worthwhile. As a result, we returned to Newfoundland for the second time in August 2016 to continue with our research and also to explore more of this enchanting part of the world.

All's well that ends well. Had it not been for our decision to stop at this small town to gas up and the suggestion by the teenage girl at the checkout register, the trip would have been unfulfilled other than having had the opportunity to see this very beautiful and picturesque Canadian province.

As you will see in the sections that follow, this document is separated into two components: Part 1—*The Duff Family*, and Part 2—*The MacKinnon Clan*. Readers need to understand that this is an overview only. I would like to think of it as a foundation or a starting point; it is certainly not all-inclusive, and is not meant to be. My purpose was simply to produce a general baseline for anyone who wants a better understanding of our family heritage. For the most part, I have restricted the lines to Nova Scotia and Newfoundland. The MacKinnons (used interchangeably with McKinnon) originated in Scotland, and the Duffs in Ireland. If anyone wishes to trace the respective families back through those countries, there are ample Ancestry-type websites available to assist.

I intend to provide this document to my cousins, siblings, and their children to do with as they wish. Some may want to provide it to their children as nice-to-know information. Others may want to build on its content and expand the trees based on the websites and databases currently available.

I might add that in structuring the two family trees in Ancestry.com, I learned of the existence of numerous other family trees that have been constructed by relatives throughout the country: some are authored by distant relatives and others by professional genealogists. If any of these linked family trees are of interest, email contact information is generally noted.

In hindsight, I can honestly say that this project has been most rewarding. Aside from the travel, I have learned so much about my ancestors and their heritage. I have also met a lot of interesting people (some distant relatives), which has brought me closer to my own family.

Enjoy the read! Hopefully you will learn something new and develop a greater appreciation for who you are.

— *Bill Duff*
November 2018

PART 1

THE DUFF FAMILY

THE EARLY YEARS

Perhaps a good starting point would be to comment on the "Orange Order," a Protestant fraternal organization based in Northern Ireland in the latter part of the eighteenth century. It was founded in County Armagh in 1795 during a period of escalating Protestant-Catholic sectarian conflict. The name was a tribute to the Dutch born Protestant King William of Orange who defeated the army of the Catholic King James II at the Battle of Boyne in 1690. Its members wore orange sashes and were referred to as "Orangemen."

From the outset, Orange gangs were responsible for driving thousands of Catholics out of their homes. Armagh was the center of the Irish linen trade, and many Catholics participated in this trade as weavers, as did many of their Protestant neighbors. The Orangemen destroyed any loom they found owned by a Catholic weaver, thereby depriving the Catholic weaver and his family of a livelihood. This situation eventually led to violent conflict such as the incident in 1795 near the village of

Loughgall where thirty Catholics were killed. No doubt this had a profound effect on any Catholic family in Ireland at the time.

Our story begins with a young boy by the name of **ARTHUR DUFF** (possibly spelled Duffe) who, at the age of 7, made the trip from Wexford, Ireland, to St. John's, Newfoundland (NL), with his mother, Mary, also known as the *Widow Duff*. (Mary's maiden name may have been Doyle, but no verification could be found.) This long voyage took place at some time between 1801 and 1810. The accommodations were far from luxurious as rumor has it that Arthur and his mother secretly stowed away aboard the ship with another Irish family, the Daltons, as they had had no financial means to make the trip. The rest of Arthur's family members, namely his siblings and father, were dead by then. It is not known how they died, but one account states that they were shot during religious uprisings in Ireland between the Protestants and Catholics. Furthermore, it was rumored that the Widow Duff always carried a gun and was reported to have said that she would shoot the first Orangeman she saw. Others thought the other family members might have died during the voyage from disease or dehydration, which was not unusual at the time.

Some descendants believe that **ARTHUR** and his mother were from Donegal in Northern Ireland but left Ireland from the port of Wexford as it was the nearest port that could accommodate the ships that were sailing to the New World. From historical records, it appears that the Duff family members were fur traders in Ireland, not weavers, which was another common trade in Ireland back then.

Once they reached Newfoundland, they landed at Holyrood, a small town some 30 miles west of the capital, St. John's. Why they landed at this location is unknown. It could have been the captain's pre-planned destination, or perhaps just the first safe haven found where they could bury those who'd died on the journey.

Loosely translated to mean "Holy Cross," Holyrood is an Irish town that is geographically located on the southern tip of Conception Bay on the Avalon Peninsula. A woman named Mary G. Veitch wrote a book titled *Come Ashore to Holyrood: A Folk History of Holyrood*. Published in 1989, the book detailed the history of this small town; the following historical excerpt is from that work:

> There are several accounts as to the origin of the name Holyrood. The term was found on John Thornton's map of Newfoundland of 1675 as being spelled "Hollyrode." There is no dispute as to the meaning of the *rode* or *rod*, but there are several theories as to how the name came to be given to Holyrood. According to E.R. Seary (register) (1971), the application of the name was not religious, but rather the name was probably transferred to the area from Holyrood House in Edinburgh in the early 1600s.
>
> There are others who feel that since the roots of the settlers were predominantly Irish Catholic, the name was in fact religious in origin. One theory that made the rounds in schoolchildren's research was that the landscape itself

suggested a cross. But regardless how it came to be, the name stuck. The local parish then adopted the cross as its name and came to be known as Holy Cross Parish.

The first recorded settlement in Holyrood began in the late 1700s and early 1800s. However, oral tradition has it that Martin O'Neil was the first settler, and that he settled in 1689. We have no evidence to either substantiate or reject that claim. However, the O'Neil property was located in the center of the main beach area, certainly a logical location for the first to arrive.

Because settlers were of Irish Catholic descent and their traditions have been so strong in this part of Conception Bay, it has always been assumed that most of the early settlers came directly from Ireland during the various waves of emigration that left that country in the 1800s. Certainly in our history there are a number of families that can trace their ancestry back to specific areas of Ireland.

As with most of the Newfoundland settlements during the 1800s, fishing was the focus of economic development. However, because Holyrood was located so far back in the bay from the inshore fishing grounds, the actual hands-on occupation of fishing was not as important. Instead, most men from the settlement worked at the Grand Bank, Western, and Labrador fisheries each summer and went seal hunting during the spring. However, bait, such as caplin and squid, were plentiful in Holyrood Harbor and contributed substantially to the local industry, not only from a procurement aspect but also to service and supply fishing vessels that came to Holyrood for bait.

The first official record found for **ARTHUR DUFF** was on the 1835 Voter's List for South Shore, Holyrood, as well as in its 1864–65 resident directory. Records indicate that in his younger years, **ARTHUR** was employed at Damson's Fishing Room in the North Arm area of Holyrood for some years as a longshoreman.[1]

In the mid-1820s, **ARTHUR** met **MARY MYERS**, a young lady from Chapel's Cove, NL, which is a small town some 10 miles northwest of Holyrood. They exchanged vows in Holyrood on January 4, 1827, a cold winter day. After their marriage, they moved to Holyrood and acquired some 300 acres of property in the "Duff's" area of Holyrood, which took its name from **ARTHUR**'s family. This parcel of land is synonymous with a small village still known as "Duff's" and lies between what is now Route 60 (Conception Bay Highway) and the Southeast Coast of Conception Bay where a thermal power plant presently exists. As of this writing, Duff's

The church that administered to the spiritual needs of the Duff family, Saints Peter and Paul Church, is in Harbour Main. It was originally built between 1811 and 1818 to serve the settlements of Holyrood, Bacon Cove, and Harbor Main.

---

1   A "fishing room" in those days was a processing center for the unloading and drying of codfish. The manual labor for this process was conducted by a "longshoreman".

Road is still in existence although no one from the original family has resided in this area for many years.

Described as a "very industrious chap," **ARTHUR** built (or purchased) a boat and started a ferryboat service across Conception Bay between Holyrood and Chapel's Cove. With the limited availability of options in its day, **ARTHUR**'s ferry service soon became a very lucrative business as it provided cost-effective transportation for people and cargo between these two developing towns.

Conception Bay and the thermal power plant that now stands adjacent to the village known as "Duff's."

Although the exact date is unknown, **ARTHUR** died sometime after 1886. His will is recorded in the Newfoundland Book of Wills (Probated in 1886). In the will, he states, in part:

> I, Arthur Duff of Holy Rood, do make this my last will and testament. I will and desire that my wife, Mary Duff, after my death become sole proprietor of all I possess making it however obligatory on her to divide as she may think fit between our six unmarried sons the land and other property at her death.

> I appoint John Kennedy and Patrick Mayers as my executors. In witness whereof, I put my hand and seal this 7th day of Jany 1870. Arthur Duff in the presence of Rev. Jeremiah O'Donnell, James X (his mark) Mayers. Patrick X (his mark) Duff. Certified correct. D.M. Browning, Registar [sic].

Chapel's Cove Landing; terminus of the Duff Ferry service on the west side of Conception Bay

ARTHUR DUFF was a very special man. After all, he was my great-great-grandfather; his eldest son was my great-grandfather **EDWARD DUFF**. In all, between 1827 and 1849, **ARTHUR** and his wife, **MARY**, had twelve children—nine sons and three daughters:

1. **EDWARD DUFF**, b. 1827.

2. **William Duff**, b. 1829.

3. **John Duff**, b. 1832.

4. **Catherine (Duff) Duggan**, b. ca. 1836.

5. **Mary (Duff) Murphy**, b. ca. 1836.

6. **Thomas Duff**, b. 1837.

7. **Matthew Duff**, b. 1838.

8. **Arthur Duff**, b. 1839.

9   **Patrick Duff**, b. 1842.

10.   **Ellen (Duff) Hicks**, b. 1844.

11.   **James Richard Duff**, b. 1846.

12.   **Peter Duff**, b. 1849.

It is interesting to note that only the six unmarried sons are mentioned in his will.

1. **EDWARD DUFF—EDWARD** was born in 1827 in Holyrood; he is my great-grandfather. **EDWARD** married **MARGARET BYRNE** who was also born in Holyrood some ten years later in 1837. Margaret was the daughter of John Byrne and Ellen Wall. John Byrne was born in Thomasville, Ireland, in 1793 and lived most of his life in Holyrood.

John Byrne's gravestone.

He passed away on January 1, 1858 and is buried in the Catholic Cemetery on the north side of Holyrood Bay.

EDWARD is listed as a fisherman in the 1864–65 Holyrood Directory. Six years later, however, he changed his occupation and tried his hand at farming as noted in the 1870–71 Directory, and he moved to the city of St. John's. Because his brother Patrick Duff (who was sixteen years younger) also listed farming in the same directory, it appears that the two brothers may have acquired land and that farming became their preferred trade.

EDWARD died on October 29, 1886 at the age of 59, when his and Margaret's last child was only 4 years old. He is buried in the Holy Cross Catholic Cemetery in Holyrood. Some of his and **MARGARET**'s children (perhaps as many as four) relocated to the Boston area. After **EDWARD**'s death, **MARGARET** went to Boston to live with their son Edward T. Duff. She died there from kidney failure on December 28, 1901 at the age of 64. Her remains were returned to Holyrood where she is buried with my great-grandfather.

EDWARD and **MARGARET** had thirteen children: my grandfather, **THOMAS J. DUFF** was number eight. (See the next chapter, "My Grandfather's Generation and the Traverse Connection" for details on **THOMAS**, his marriage, and children.)

The gravestone for Edward and Margaret Duff.

2. **William Duff**—Little is known about Edward's brother William, who was born in 1829. In the 1864–65 Holyrood Directory, William is listed as a fisherman, but he is not noted in any of the other directories. According to the baptismal records for Saints Peter and Paul Catholic

Church in Harbour Main (near Chapel's Cove),[2] William Duff and Ellen Crawley had an illegitimate son named William (oh, oh!) Duff on August 20, 1875. It is believed that William (the father) never married and worked aboard ships his entire life. He eventually died in an English sailor's home in London.

3. **John Duff**—John was born in Holyrood in 1832. There is a baptismal record at Saints Peter and Paul Catholic Church in Harbour Main for John's illegitimate daughter, Mary, who was born out of wedlock on January 19, 1858 to Elisa Hawco. Mary's godparents are listed as Michael Hawco and Mary Sliney. There is also a baptismal record for a Bridget Duff, the daughter of John Duff and a woman named Mary, who was born in December 1859.

After at least two illegitimate children, John finally married Frances Neal on May 12, 1867 at Saints Peter and Paul Catholic Church in Harbour Main. Frances's family originated from Parish Bally Mucaddy, County Cork, Ireland. The marriage was presided over by Rev. Kyran Walsh and witnessed by William Maher and Ellen Ryan.

John was a fisherman off and on his entire life. He was listed as such in the 1864–65 Holyrood Directory and again in the 1894–95 McAlpine's

---

2   The parish of Saints Peter and Paul Catholic Church in Harbour Main covered not only Holyrood but the neighboring communities as well. Due to the distance and the available transportation (horse-drawn wagon), it was customary for the priest to travel to the congregation and not vice-versa. The Rev. Kyran Walsh was assigned to Saints Peter and Paul and was continuously traveling to attend to the spiritual needs of his parishioners. The church still has an active congregation to this day.

Directory. However, it appears he did a brief stint at farming in the interim as he was listed as a farmer residing in North Arm, Holyrood in the Lovell's 1871 Directory. John died of gangrene on September 8, 1912 at the age of 80.

His wife, Frances, died on February 25, 1895 and was buried in the Holy Cross Catholic Cemetery in Holyrood. It is interesting to note the other names that are inscribed on her headstone: John MacKay (age 27) and John Cunningham (age 37) from County Tipperary, Ireland, both of whom were lost at sea on October 11, 1865.

Frances Duff's gravestone.

4. **Catherine (Duff) Duggan**—Catherine was born in 1836 in Holyrood as were all of her siblings. In 1860, she married Thomas Duggan (of Holyrood) at Saints Peter and Paul Catholic Church in Harbour Main. In the various local directories covering the period 1870 through 1897, Thomas Duggan was listed both as a fisherman and a farmer living in North Arm, Holyrood. Thomas and Catherine had eight children. Following Catherine's death in 1871, Thomas remarried and moved to Placentia, NF (some 50 miles to the west), where he continued his life as a fisherman. Thomas and his second wife had four more children.

5. **Mary (Duff) Murphy**—One of Edward's younger sisters, Mary Duff was born in Holyrood in 1836. In 1856, Mary married John Murphy who was the son of Edward and Mary (Dobbin) Murphy. John was listed as a fisherman in the 1864–65 Holyrood Directory.

John and Mary had four children: Catherine Murphy (born 1857), Ellen Murphy (born 1859), Bridget Murphy (born 1861), and Michael Murphy (born 1863).

Following the death of her husband, Mary married a man named John Kennedy on February 22, 1873 at Saints Peter and Paul Catholic Church in Harbour Main. No children resulted from Mary's second marriage.

6. **Thomas Duff**—Edward's brother Thomas was born in Holyrood in 1837. When he was 30 years of age, he married Ellen McGrath of McGrath's Road in Holyrood on February 10, 1867. Ellen was three years his junior. The ceremony was administered by Rev. Kyran Walsh at Saints Peter and Paul Catholic Church in Harbour Main. Although Thomas was listed as a fisherman in the directories of 1870 and 1894–97, like his brothers, he later took up farming as noted in the 1898 and 1904 Holyrood directories.

In Mary Veitch's book, *Come Ashore to Holyrood: A Folk History of Holyrood*, Ellen McGrath is described as a skilled midwife. She practiced "midwifery" during the time her own family was growing up. Ellen is said to have "borned" over 500 babies during her lifetime.[3]

---

3   In colonial North America, the typical woman gave birth to her children at home. While female relatives and neighbors clustered at the bedside to offer support and encouragement, most women were assisted in childbirth by a midwife. Midwives were typically older women who relied on the practical experience they received in having delivered many children. Skilled midwives were highly valued.

Thomas died on October 15, 1912 at the age of 75. He is buried in the Holy Cross Catholic Cemetery in Holyrood. His will as listed in the Newfoundland Book of Wills reads as follows:

> I, Thomas Duff of Holyrood Conception Bay, being of sound mind and memory, do make my last will and testament this 6th day of September, the year of our Lord 1900.
>
> First, I give and bequeath to my wife Ellen my dwelling house and all it contains, one cow, two sheep, my horse, carriage, all carts and farming utensils. My said wife is to divide all the above mention [sic] to my sons as she may think proper. The cabbage garden and my out house [sic] is to be my wife's also. She is to divide them as mention [sic] before.
>
> Second, my land being on both sides of the road leading to Indian Pond the land inside is bound by Pat Duff's land on the N. and by Ed Duff's land on the S. Outside by Pat Duff on both sides also pice [piece of?] land lying inside of my brother Patt's fence containing about one acre one eight (1/8) of it tilled. My land being by the road leading to Main line of road conting [sic] about five acres and bound by Arthur Duggan on the south also a small garden at the angle of road next Patt Duff's land also piece of land about sixty feet more or less by railway track bound by Patt Duff on the South and by Sea Shore on the North, and Pat Duff

on the west. All these lands is [sic] to be divided between my three sons if they return home and remain, but if not come or remain: it is only for him or them that will come and remain.

Third, I will and bequeath to my daughter Ellen one sheep, this year or next or when she may demand it. My nephey [sic] Arthur Duggan is have my lauch [boat?] until my son or sons come to use it.

I hereby set my hand and seal

    Thomas his X mark Duff

    In presence Michl Rourk, James Butler,

    Certified correct D.M. Browning, Registrar

    Granted to Ellen Duff on the 12th day of Dec. 1906. Value of Est. $800 [*very faint*]

If this will does not appear to be perfectly clear, it isn't. It would be a nightmare to decipher exactly what Thomas had in mind. But it illustrates how illiterate settlers relied entirely on local officials, in this case Mr. Browning, to convey their wishes.

In the 1921 census, the Widow Ellen Duff was residing at Duff's in Holyrood with her daughter, Ellen B. Walsh, born in 1878, and also a widow. After her first husband (Joseph Walsh) passed away, she later married William Kennedy, who was a lighthouse keeper in Harbour

Main. Thomas's widow, Ellen, died on January 14, 1925 at the age of 84 and was buried with Thomas at the Holy Cross Cemetery in Holyrood.

7. **Matthew Duff**—Another of Edward's brothers, Matthew was born in Holyrood in 1838 and married Mary MacKay in Saints Peter and Paul Catholic Church in 1867 when he was 29. Matthew was listed in the 1870 Alpine's Directory as a fisherman; he died of "consumption" in 1905. Though Matthew died at age 67, death by consumption was one of the most common killers of young adults in the nineteenth century. It is now commonly known as tuberculosis.

After Matthew's death, his wife, Mary, moved to Roxbury, MA, where she passed away in 1907. Her death announcement was listed in the *Daily News* on February 8, 1907 as follows:

> Mrs. Mary Duff, formerly Miss MacKay, died in Roxbury, Mass on January 23, and was buried from her late residence, 214 Cabot Street, on January 26th. High Mass was celebrated at the Church of St. Francis de Sales. The late Mrs. Duff has relatives in this city.

Matthew and Mary had seven (7) children.

8. **Arthur Duff**—Arthur was born in Holyrood in 1839. He married Anne Grace of Salmon Cove in 1874. They moved to Boston, MA, for a number of years, but never had any children. Arthur died in 1912 of blood poisoning at the age of 72.

9. **Patrick Duff**—Patrick was born in September 1842 in Holyrood. In the book previously referenced (*Come Ashore to Holyrood . . .* by Mary Veitch), we learn about the ferry service that the Duffs operated. Ms. Veitch wrote:

> In 1851, it was determined that the shortest time and the best route to take in order to deliver the mail from St. John's to Carbonear by horse was to do it in three stages. The first was from St. John's to Floods, Holyrood; the second was from Chapel's Cove to Brigus and the third was from Brigus to Carbonear. The mail came as far as John's Flood's on the southside of Holyrood. The Holyrood and area mail was taken for delivery and the rest was taken half a mile further [sic] to 'Ferry.' Here the mail was taken by ferry boat [sic] to Chapel's Cove where it continued on the remaining two stages of its journey.
>
> The ferry service to Chapel's Cove was initially provided by Patrick and James Duff who built their homes near the ferry boat [sic] site. They used to row boats for the service. They could only accommodate two to four passengers at a crossing.

The Duffs were later joined by Arthur Duggan, Martin Myers and Patrick Corbett, all from Chapel's Cove. They built homes nearby, thus creating a new neighborhood known as Duff's Road.

In November 1884, the railway went through from St. John's to Harbour Grace and the Duff's ferry service became obsolete. Because the Duff men had initiated the ferry service, the name Ferry was changed to Duff's. When the train passed through, it made a short stop over there. Some people could catch the train or get off there; and the spot became known as "Duff's siding."

Old railroad station site in Holyrood which sits on the southern rim of Conception Bay, and is adjacent to the Station Diner.

Duff's died out when the trains came and made the ferry unnecessary. Duff's "siding" died out again with the demise of passenger trains. In 1970 the area of Duff's again became important, not just to Holyrood, but to the entire province of Newfoundland. This was due to the construction of an electrical generating station at Duff's. The three 300-foot-high smokestacks of the generating station at Duff's can be seen for miles around across Conception Bay.

In the 1870–71 directories, both Patrick and my great-grandfather Edward were listed as farmers living on Freshwater Road in St. John's. According to the 1904 directory, Patrick moved back to Holyrood to continue farming and lived with his brother, James, at the Duff's.

Patrick never married. He died in 1933 at age 90 and was buried with his brother James in Holyrood. Rumor has it that he broke his back lifting an anchor shortly before his death.

10. **Ellen Duff**—Edward's sister Ellen was born in Holyrood in 1844. She married Joseph Hicks in 1874 and had eight (8) children. She died in 1916 and is buried in the Holy Cross Catholic Cemetery in Holyrood.

11. **James Richard Duff**— In 1846, when my great-grandfather was 19 years of age, his younger brother James was born to the Duffs. James married Bridget LaCour in 1896 and had three children. He died in 1925 and his wife, Bridget, passed in 1940 at the age of 74.

When James died at Duff's, his funeral was well attended. But what was particularly unique was the obituary that was printed in the local newspaper (author unknown). Following is a transcription that illustrates how it captured the tenor of the times and the flowery language that so beautifully depicts the passing of an Irish Catholic faithful.

> On Good Friday, April 10, the angel of death entered quietly the home and snapped from the midst of loved ones the soul of James Duff, one of the most highly esteemed residents of Duff's and a man who was greatly admired and dearly loved by all who had the privilege of his personal acquaintance. Death meant for him the ending of a good Christian life, spent in bringing cheer and comfort to others and in the performance of those many acts and unselfish kindness and charity, which characterizes a highly successful and useful early existence. He was a thoroughly devoted member of his church [that] meant so much to him during his whole lifetime. And which gave him strength and courage to cheerfully resign his soul to its maker when the final summons came to him in his 79th year of his age.
>
> Sprung from good old Irish stock, Arthur Duff, who

[e]migrated from Wexford almost a century and a quarter ago, and having been employed as an Irish "youngster" upon the fishing plantation of Sampson's, North Arm, Holyrood, he married Mary Myers, of Chapel's Cove and settled at the East Point of Holyrood Harbor. He was the pioneer settler at Duff's, which bears and honors the name of its founder today. From the forest primeral [Arthur] built up a fishing and farming homestead and raised the large family of nine sons and three daughters.

But one survives today: Patrick, in his 85th year—hale and hearty and able to walk from Holyrood to Duff's, a distance of five miles. James Duff possessed a strong, healthy and robust constitution and in the cod and seal fisheries of the 60's and 70's, and early 80's, he was held to be a leader and expert worker. His capability was recognized in those industries by the late Hon. Samuel Blanford and Captains Adam and Fairweather, of the Dundee sealing ships. A swift walker, the distance to Duff's was regarded as trifling to him, and it was a rare occasion in his palmy days he was absent from Sunday Mass. Several years ago, the deceased developed bronchial and lung troubles, and since then had not enjoyed his usual good health; and although complaining for a few months, his condition was not considered serious until a month ago. All that medical attention and kindness could do to alleviate his sufferings was done, but to no avail. God called him to this heavenly home. He was visited during his illness by his beloved Pastor, Father Finn, who prepared his soul for its exit from this world. His funeral took place on Easter Sunday from his late residence to the beautiful Southside Cemetery. The Star of the Sea Association, of which he was a charter member, attended in processional order and in full strength the obsequies of their brother member, and the number attending from Hr. Main, Chapel's Cove, and South Shore so greatly swelled the procession that the funeral was the largest in the history of Duff's.

The funeral service was read at the home and final absolution given at the grave side by the Rev. Fr. Finn, P.P., after which the remains of James Duff were reverently laid in his grave by his brother members under the direction of Mr. Theophilus LaCour, who had charge of the funeral arrangements. At the regular quarterly meeting of the Star of the Sea Association, held on Sunday last, a vote of sympathy was passed and ordered to be sent to the widow, Mrs. Bridget Duff, and family, together with the benefit of $40. Surviving him are his widow, two sons, Peter and Arthur, and one daughter, Mrs. Morgan, and a loving and loyal brother, Patrick, of whom deep and sincere sympathy is felt.—R.I.P.

12. **Peter Duff**—The youngest of Arthur Duff's children, Peter was born in 1849 at Duff's, Holyrood, and eventually settled in the small town of Topsail which is about 15 miles northeast of Holyrood. He married Mary King from Bell Island, NL, and had ten children. Peter worked in the seal industry and died in 1921 at the age of 72.

My grandfather **THOMAS J. DUFF** (b. 1873[4]) was the eighth child of thirteen (13) born to **EDWARD DUFF** and **MARGARET BYRNE**. He had seven (7) sisters and five (5) brothers:

1. **Mary Duff,** b. 1858.

2. **Catherine Duff,** b. 1861.

3. **Emma Duff,** b. 1863.

4. **Arthur Joseph Duff,** b. 1865.

5. **Minnie Duff,** b. 1867.

---

4   Thomas J. Duff's birth year is listed as 1872 on his gravestone, but as 1873 in the 1900 census.

6.   **Emma Duff**, b. 1870.

7.   **Bridget Bernard Duff**, b. 1872.

8.   **John Joseph Duff**, b. 1872.

9.   **THOMAS J. DUFF**, b. 1873.

10.   **Edward T. Duff**, b. 1875.

11.   **Patrick Francis Duff**, b. 1878.

12.   **William Joseph Duff**, b. 1880.

13.   **Margaret Duff**, b. 1882.

With the exception of John Joseph Duff (b. 1872) and Edward T. Duff (b. 1875), little is known of my grandfather's other siblings. What is interesting to note, however, is the connection between the **Duff** family and the **Condon** family.

Originally from Ireland, the Condons settled in the Caplin Bay area of Newfoundland, which is about 45 miles north of St. John's. Kyran Condon (b. 1831) married Ellen Downey (b. 1839) from St. John's, in 1863. They had numerous children, including three daughters:

1.   **Margaret Condon**, b. 1863.

2.   **Alice J. Condon**, b. 1869.

3.   **MARY F. CONDON**, b. 1863 (who married my grandfather **THOMAS J. DUFF** in 1895.)

Mary (Condon) Duff in Newfoundland field with an unknown friend.

1. **Margaret Condon**—Mary's sister **Margaret** was also born in 1863 in St. John's. She died in Dorchester, MA, in 1924. In 1884, Margaret married **Thomas Traverse** of Carbonear, NL, and had six children, one of whom was John Traverse (b. 1889) who later married Anastasia Sullivan (b. 1897). Thomas Traverse was nicknamed "Tommie" and had a street named after him in Coachman's Cove (400 miles northwest of St. John), which was called "Tommie's Lane" and was situated next to his house and the local cemetery. Tommie immigrated to the US in 1914 and

resided in Neponset, MA. According to his grandson, Tommie worked for the Stearns Lumber Company for a number of years as a "teamster."[5]

Note: Margaret and Tommie's son, John, also had a son John Traverse (b. 1921), but he went by the nickname "Jack." Jack owned and operated an insurance company in Dorchester, MA, and was a frequent visitor to our home in Milton. He handled most, if not all, of our family's insurance needs. Although my father always described Jack as his "cousin," in reality, it was Jack's father, John Traverse (b. 1889) who was my father's first cousin. After Jack died in 1981, his two sons, Paul and John Traverse, and Paul's son Michael developed the family insurance business and added real estate services. It is now called JW Traverse Companies and is located in Milton, MA.

2. **Alice J. Condon**—Born in 1869, **Alice**, the middle sister, married my grandfather's brother, **John Joseph Duff** (b. 1872) in 1894. This was not a common occurrence where two sisters married two brothers. Nonetheless, "Jack" Duff, as he was known, was a true entrepreneur who became one of the more interesting and colorful members of my grandfather's family. In 1889, Jack moved to St. John's and joined the Royal Newfoundland Constabulary (RNC), which at that time provided police services to the communities of St. John's and the Northeast Avalon Peninsula. This employment was confirmed by the 1890 edition of the

---

5   Originally called the A. T. Stearns Co., Stearns Lumber was a large lumber processing facility that covered some 14 acres. It was located on the Neponset River on a site formerly part of Port Norfolk, which had been pastureland prior to the nineteenth century.

Might & Co. Directory of St. John's, which lists him as a "constable" residing at Ft. Townhead, St. John's, with his widowed mother, Margaret, who was employed as a "confectioner."[6]

The RNC dates back to 1729 with the appointment of the first police constables, making it the oldest civil police force in North America. It was modeled after the Royal Irish Constabulary and continues to serve alongside the Royal Canadian Mounted Police, which is contracted by the provincial government to provide provincial and community police services. The RNC services mainly major metropolitan areas, while the RCMP serves smaller and remote rural areas.

In the early 1890s, after a brief stint as a grocer, rumor has it that Jack Duff headed to Colorado to try his hand in the gold mining business. However, the timeline is sketchy as this was many years after the original Colorado Rush, which had begun in 1858 and lasted until roughly the creation of the Colorado Territory in 1861. During that time, about 100,000 gold seekers took part in one of the greatest gold rushes in North American history.

The Colorado gold rush, which followed approximately a decade after the California Gold Rush, was accompanied by a dramatic influx of immigrants to the region of the Rocky Mountains and was exemplified by the phrase "Pikes Peak or Bust," a reference to the mountain in the Front Range that guided many early prospectors to the region westward over the Great Plains.

---

6   A person who makes or sells sweets or chocolates.

If Jack Duff didn't make his fortune in Colorado, there were other "gold rushes" going on at the time in which he may have profited. One was the Klondike Gold Rush in Canada's Yukon Territory (1896–99), another was the Hope Gold Rush in Alaska, which hit its peak during the mid-1890s.

Nonetheless, it's unclear where and how Jack Duff acquired his wealth, but when he returned to Newfoundland, he purchased several real estate properties in St. John's, including his future residence, Thornlea Cottage, a very prestigious home on Waterford Bridge Road in St. John's. His next endeavor was to purchase movie theaters in St. John's, as the popularity of motion pictures was surging at that time. One of the theaters he purchased was the Nickel Theater, which earned him the nickname "Nickel Jack." He was also known as "JJ."

The 1927 edition of the directory "Who's Who in and from Newfoundland" described him in this manner:

> Duff, John Joseph—Proprietor Queen Theatre, Water Street, St. John's West; born October 22nd 1867 at Holyrood, the son of Edward and Margaret (Byrne) Duff, Educated at Holyrood. Established provision and grocery business, Water Street, St. John's, 1895. Started moving picture theatre, 1910. Expanded business and established the New Queen Theatre, one of the most modern in the city, in 1926. Married 1894, to Alice J. Condon. Children: one son and one daughter. Societies: K of C, Benevolent Irish Society Club; Benevolent Irish. Recreations: Motoring and

fishing. Religion: Roman Catholic. Politics: Independent. Residence: Westmount, St. John's West; Summer residence: Waterford Valley, St. John's West, Nfld.

Jack Duff was also mentioned in Paul O'Neill's book, *The Oldest City: the Story of St. John's Newfoundland* with the following:

> In 1927 JJ Duff erected the Duff Building on Water Street, opposite Steer's Cove. The lobby of the building led to the Queen movie house, at the back, on George Street. The theatre had a striking proscenium stage and was a vast cinema. During World War II, the Queen came under the management of the Nickel. It was renovated as the York Theatre, and became a second-run house for features that played the Nickel the previous week. When it finally closed its doors, the Queen, or York, was taken over by Steer's and it became a warehouse. The St. John's Convention Center later occupied the site.

Jack and Alice Duff didn't have any biological children, but adopted a daughter, Nellie, in 1904 and a son, Cecil, in 1910. Jack died in 1940 and is buried in the Belvedere Cemetery in St. John's. Buried with him is his wife, Alice (Condon) Duff, who died in 1953 in Toronto, Ontario.

Gravestone of Jack and Alice Duff.

3. **MARY CONDON**—Probably envisioning better opportunities in America, in 1890, my grandfather **THOMAS J. DUFF** emigrated from Holyrood to Boston. Five years later in 1895, his future wife, **MARY CONDON**, also moved to Boston where they married the same year.

According to the 1900 U.S. Census, **THOMAS J. DUFF** originally lived at 118 Winthrop St., Boston, which is now in the Roxbury section near Dudley Square. It is interesting to note that my grandmother apparently took great liberty in adjusting her age to suit the occasion. Accordingly, it does not seem inappropriate that in that census, instead of her correct date of birth, 1869, it is listed as April's Fools Day, 1863, almost ten years before her husband's birth date of 1873.

The 1900 U.S. Census states, in part:

> …Thomas J. Duff was born in 1873, had been married for four years, moved to the U.S. in 1890 from Canada, was employed as a steamfitter, and can read, write, and speak English. The record continues to note that Mary F. (Condon) Duff was 25 years of age, had been married for four years, was the mother of two children, moved to the U.S. in 1895, and can read, write, and speak English. The two children were Marguerite J. Duff, a daughter, born in 1896, and Arthur G. Duff, a son, born in 1897.

The 1930 U.S. Census added:

> …that a cousin, Alice McGrath,* age 29, also resided in the same household. She is described as a single woman who moved to the U.S. from Newfoundland in 1918. She is employed as a nurse who can read, write, and speak English; both parents were from Newfoundland.
>
> *Alice Josephine McGrath (b. 1896) was the daughter of Elizabeth "Bessie" (Duff) McGrath (b. 1873) and the granddaughter of Thomas Duff (b. 1837), who was my great-grandfather **EDWARD**'s brother.*

As I mentioned in the *Preface*, during the course of this family project, my wife, Leigh, and I traveled to Newfoundland on two occasions (2014 and 2016) and were fortunate to meet two wonderful people who are my distant cousins. The first was Joe Byrne of Holyrood and the second, Alice Lee Finn (b. 1938) who lives in St. John's. Both are a treasure trove of family information and are directly responsible for most of the content of this limited history.

When we first met Alice at her home in St. John's, she greeted me at the door like I had known her my entire life. She then presented me with the only photo I had at the time of my grandfather with his brother Jack Duff taken in the early 1920s. She couldn't wait to say: "It may surprise you to know that you look just like your grandfather." Truly, a priceless photograph!

Nellie Duff, Jack Duff, Cecil Duff, Catherine McGrath, and my grandfather, Tom Duff, c. 1920.

Alice Finn's mother is Catherine "Kitty" McGrath (b. 1899) and her aunt (Kitty's sister) is Alice J. McGrath. After her grandmother (Bessie Duff) died in 1947, Alice Finn left St. John's at age 17 and moved with her mother to Jamaica Plain, MA. At that time, Alice J. McGrath was living nearby with my grandparents on Neponset Ave. in Dorchester, MA; she was listed as a "cousin" in the 1930 census. (Because Alice Finn's aunt lived with my grandparents, she got to know them and has provided details about them I otherwise would not have known.) Alice Finn didn't return to St. John's until 1963. As my grandfather died in

1944 and my grandmother in 1952, Alice Finn is the only relative alive today who has any recollection of Thomas and "Aunt Mary," as she called my grandmother. Simply put, Alice Finn's great-grandfather Thomas was my great-grandfather **EDWARD**'s brother.

In addition to my grandfather **THOMAS**'s move to Massachusetts, other family members followed suit. Although the records are scarce, it appears that at least one of his brothers, Edward T. Duff (b. 1875), and two sisters, Catherine (Duff) Keating (b. 1861) who settled in Roxbury, MA, and Margaret (Duff) O'Brien (b. 1882) of Neponset, made the trip.

After my great-grandfather **EDWARD** passed away in 1886, my great-grandmother **MARGARET** travelled to Boston where she died in 1901. At the time of her death, she resided at 32 Bower St., Boston, which is now part of Roxbury. It may have been a nursing home or hospital at the time.

One of my grandfather's younger brothers, Edward T. Duff (b. 1875), immigrated to the United States in September 1900, about ten years after my grandfather. In 1903, he married Ellen Murphy from the Boston area, and the couple had five children. On his immigration form, Edward T. noted his address as 132 Winthrop St. in Boston, just a few doors down from 118 Winthrop St. where my grandfather was residing. Several years later, the

Gravestone of Edward and Ellen Duff.

1910 U.S. Census noted that he was a store clerk living at 18 Sewall St. Boston. When he died in 1923 at the young age of 49, Edward T. was working as a bartender at a "saloon in Boston." He is buried in the New Calvary Cemetery in Mattapan, MA, along with his wife, Ellen (d. 1945), and a Catherine A. Sullivan (d. 1972). The relationship with the Duff family is unknown.

T.J. DUFF AND COMPANY

AFTER MY GRANDPARENTS **THOMAS J.** and **MARY (CONDON) DUFF** were married in 1895, they appeared to move every few years, most likely to accommodate their burgeoning family. The first to be born was my aunt Marguerite, followed by Arthur Gordon. At that time, they were living at 118 Winthrop St. in Boston where my grandfather was working as a "steamfitter."[7]

By the time they moved again, that time to 16 Bowman St. in Boston, three more children had arrived: Kenneth John, Vivian Mary, and my father, **EDWARD JOSEPH DUFF**.

Following is a list of **THOMAS** and **MARY**'s children with their birth dates:

1. **Marguerite Duff**, b. 1896.

2. **Arthur Gordon Duff**, b. 1897.

---

7   One who installs and repairs pipes in heating and refrigeration systems.

3.   **Kenneth John Duff**, b. 1900.

4.   **Vivian Mary Duff**, b. 1904.

5.   **EDWARD JOSEPH DUFF**, b. 1906.

The first house they owned was a white, two-story frame structure at 240 Neponset Ave. in Dorchester opposite St. Ann Catholic Church. This became their home around 1920 and would be the only home they would ever own.

The Thomas and Mary (Condon) Duff family home at 240 Neponset Ave. in Dorchester.

1920 passport photo of Thomas J. Duff.

Although he had been a steamfitter for many years, my grandfather didn't own his business until 1936. T. J. Duff and Company was located at 628 Harrison Ave. in what is now Roxbury. He continued to work in the plumbing business until he passed away on October 9, 1944 at the age of 70. He and my grandmother are buried at St. Joseph's Cemetery in W. Roxbury, MA.

1. **Marguerite J. Duff**—The oldest child, Marguerite, who was born in 1896, married **Walter F. Como** in 1922. Originally from Gloucester, MA, Walter was a bookkeeper by trade and did a brief stint with the U.S. Army during World War I.

They had one child, **Marjorie A. Como**, who was born in 1925. Various sources indicate that Marjorie was a very attractive and talented young lady who landed a variety of modeling positions. It is rumored that she held the title of "Miss Filenes" (Boston's premier department store) during the 1940s; it was not uncommon to see her image on highway billboard signs throughout the Boston area advertising the popular beverage Coca-Cola. A graduate of Regis College, Marjorie eventually settled in Washington, D.C. and took a position with the Internal Revenue Service. Shortly thereafter, she married Sam W. Clark Jr., a Dallas attorney, who was a cousin of Ramsey Clark, the U.S. Attorney General at that time. Marjorie died of cancer in 1974 at age 49.

42

Gravestone of Marguerite and Walter Como.

Marguerite and Walter Como eventually moved to Scituate where she died in 1977 at the age of 80. Her husband, Walter, died in 1986 in Barnstable, MA, of a heart attack. He was 88 years of age. All three are buried at the Fairview Cemetery in Scituate. Unfortunately, I never had the opportunity to meet any of them.

2. **Arthur Gordon Duff**—My oldest uncle, Arthur, was born in 1897. A die-hard bachelor, Uncle Arthur spent most of his life in California, specifically San Diego.

Before settling in California, Arthur apparently travelled internationally on several occasions. His passport application, submitted in 1920, asked for periods of time outside of the U.S. He responded with the notation "France . . . AEP (possibly AEF) from 1918 to 1919." This could be interpreted to mean military service with the American Expeditionary Forces, which was the expeditionary force of the United States Army during World War I, established on July 5, 1917, in France under the command

Arthur G. Duff, 1919.

of Gen. John J. Pershing. During the United States campaign in World War I, AEF fought alongside French and British troops against the German Empire. Unfortunately, no other supporting documentation citing Arthur's connection to it could be found.

Nonetheless, by 1920, Arthur was working for a steamship company in Manhattan known as the "New York and Cuba Mail Steamship Company." Having been attached to the Rotterdam office of that company, he traveled extensively to a variety of countries that included Cuba, Holland, Spain, France, and Belgium. By the late 1920s, he moved to Los Angeles where he lived and worked as an accountant. At some point, he moved further south in California to San Diego where he spent the rest of his life.

As with Aunt Marguerite, I never met Uncle Arthur. But I do remember his reputation to be considerate, meticulous, and kind. Like clockwork, Arthur would send all of us (my brothers, sisters, and me) a Christmas card and a check year after year during the 1950s and early 1960s. He was like the proverbial Santa Claus—you never saw him, but you knew he was there. Apparently, he worked his entire life as an accountant and "almost" married a few times, but never wished the commitment. He died in 1967 at age 70 and is buried with my grandparents in W. Roxbury, MA.

3. **Kenneth John Duff**—The second son of **THOMAS** and **MARY DUFF** was my "Uncle Ken," who was born at the turn of the century in 1900. A heating engineer, he lived with his parents on Neponset Ave. in Dorchester until he married **Abby Elizabeth Cummings** in 1924. They eventually had four children: **Kenneth Duff Jr.** (b. 1925), **Thomas Duff** (b. 1929), **Jacqueline Duff** (b. 1935), and **Maureen Duff** (b. 1942). After living in Dorchester on North Munroe Terrace for several years, Uncle Ken and Aunt Abby did what many young families did at the time—they moved to the suburbs. They had scraped together almost $5,000 and bought a small house on Lawrence Road in Milton. This home was in the same neighborhood where my father, **EDWARD**, would eventually buy his first home in 1937.

Although Aunt Abby passed away in 1976 at the age of 74, Uncle Ken outlived all of his siblings and died in 1999 just months before his 100th birthday! Both he and Abby are buried in their family plot at the Milton Cemetery.

In 2008, my cousin Tom died where he lived on Cape Cod to be followed by his wife, Mary (Cotter), less than a year later.

Kenneth Jr. had moved to Los Angeles many years earlier and worked in various retail businesses. He

Gravestone of Kenneth and Abby Duff.

eventually settled in the Beverly Hills area of Los Angeles until he passed away in 2016 at the age of 92. He never married.

My cousins, Jacqueline (Duff) Sefton and Maureen (Duff) Parks still live with their respective spouses in Canton, MA.

4. **Vivian Mary Duff**—After a short courtship, my Aunt Vivian (b. 1904) married Francis Carroll Dunn in 1926. The couple then had two children: Delores (aka "Dottie" Dunn) born in 1929, and William T. Dunn (b.1934). Uncle Carroll was born in Hyde Park, MA in 1901. His father, William T. Dunn (b. 1871), was a blacksmith from Blackstone, MA on the state line just north of Providence, Rhode Island. At that time, the family resided on Milton Avenue in Hyde Park, MA. The 1940 U.S. Census shows that Uncle Carroll (as we knew him) was working as a salesman for a leather company. He died of a heart attack in 1967 just shy of his 67th birthday. Vivian eventually moved to Randolph, MA, where she lived with her daughter. She died in 1987 of cardiogenic shock at the age of 83. They are both buried at the Fairview Cemetery in Scituate, MA.

Carroll and Vivian's daughter, Delores "Dottie" Dunn married and divorced Jack Marshall, then later married Ernest J. Arceneaux who died in 2014. After

Francis Carroll and Vivian Dunn's gravestone.

moving to Exeter, NH, in 2013, Delores died three years later in 2016. Her brother, William T. "Billy" Dunn, worked for the New England Telephone Company most of his life. He lived in North Ft. Myers, Florida with his wife, Joette, until his passing in 2018.

5. **Edward "Eddy" Duff**—My father, **EDWARD JOSEPH DUFF**, was born 1906 in Boston, the youngest child of **TOM** and **MARY DUFF**. Witty with a tremendous sense of humor, he often credited the 1906 San Francisco Earthquake with the year of his birth. **EDWARD** lived with his parents on Neponset Ave. in Dorchester, opposite St. Ann Catholic Church and school. In 1924 he enrolled at Fisher's Business College in Boston and learned the skills necessary to become a stenographer. He left after approximately one year apparently to enlist in the U.S. Coast Guard, which he did in 1926. He remained on active duty for some five years and was discharged in 1931. In 1935, he moved to Milton and lived with my Uncle Ken on Lawrence Road until he bought his own home on Fuller's Lane in Milton in 1937, the year he married my mother, **ALICE C. McKINNON**.

Edward J. Duff

Edward J. Duff, 1930.

The McKinnon family home at 242 Neponset Ave., Dorchester.

Growing up, my father literally lived next door to the McKinnons at 242 Neponset Ave. in Dorchester. As noted later, my grandfather **HUGH MCKINNON** and his wife, **ANNE B. (LOCKE) MCKINNON** had six (6) children in that house, the oldest of whom was my mother, **ALICE CHRISTINA MCKINNON** (b. 1908). It's not known how long my parents courted, but on April 2, 1937, my father married the girl next door and bought her to his home at 49 Fuller's Lane in Milton, two blocks away from my Uncle Ken's house. The Fuller's Lane house was a lovely white Dutch Colonial on a corner lot across from Cunningham Park. The entrance to the driveway was framed by two large sugar maple trees; a babbling brook ran through the property and under an arched wooden bridge that matched the accent colors of the house, certainly a pleasant change from the gritty neighborhood along Neponset Avenue.

Over a period of thirty years, my father held a variety of positions from running a produce stand in East Milton Square to a career as a union longshoreman on the docks of the Boston waterfront.[8]

---

8   He was primarily employed by Atlantic & Gulf Stevedores, Inc. in Boston. The term stevedore was originally synonymous with a longshoreman or dockworker, which were terms for a manual laborer involved in the loading or unloading of ships. After the shipping container revolution of the 1950s, the number of dockworkers required decreased by over 90 percent and "stevedore" increasingly came to mean a stevedoring firm that contracts with a port, ship owner, or charterer to load or unload a vessel.

THE CHILDREN OF
EDWARD "EDDY" AND
ALICE (MCKINNON) DUFF

My parents had six (6) children; they were born between 1937 and 1949: five in the first six years, and then . . . me.

1. **Edward F. Duff,** b. late 1937.

2. **Virginia M. Duff,** b. 1939.

3. **Robert J. Duff,** b. 1940.

4. **Alice C. Duff,** b. 1942.

5. **Margaret A. Duff,** b. 1943.

6. **WILLIAM H. DUFF,** b. 1949.

1. **Edward F. Duff**—My brother, Edward, was the firstborn, arriving in late 1937. After four years in the U.S. Navy, Ed held a variety of jobs until 1975 when he bought a neighborhood bar in Dorchester known as the Leedsville Café. He operated this establishment until he was diagnosed with liver cancer early in 1999. He passed away later that year just before his 62nd birthday. He and his wife, Pat, had two sons, though at some point they divorced.

A proud Mom with her three sons: Edward, me, and Robert at my sister Alice's wedding in 1962

2. **Virginia M. Duff**—My oldest sister, "Ginny," came next in 1939. Ginny went to high school at the Fontbonne Academy in Milton, which was operated by the Sisters of St. Joseph of Boston. Tragically, Ginny's life was snuffed out in 1957 resulting from an automobile accident on the Jamaicaway in Boston. She was only 18.

3. **Robert J. Duff**—My parents' second son was born in 1940. At age 21, Bob enlisted in the U.S. Army for two years. In 1964, he was fortunate to be hired by the New England Telephone and Telegraph Company where he worked for some forty-five years. In 1975, he partnered with my brother Ed to buy and operate the Leedsville Café, a neighborhood bar in Dorchester, but on a part time basis. Bob and his wife, Marie, have four children and live in Milton.

4. **Alice C. (Duff) Doherty**—Alice was born in 1942 and also attended Fontbonne Academy in Milton. "Blondie," as everyone calls her, was married in 1961 and had three children. Divorced from her first husband, she remarried and later became a widow. She recently retired from the State of Massachusetts where she was the manager of the Braintree, MA, Department of Motor Vehicles Office. She resides in Braintree with her two sons and granddaughter.

5. **Margaret A. (Duff) Smith**—My third sister, "Peggy," was born in 1943. Like her sisters, Peggy attended Fontbonne Academy in Milton and married in 1962. Divorced, widowed, and remarried, she has four children and resides in Charlotte, NC.

6. **WILLIAM H. DUFF**—Because I was born in 1949, I'm sure you can now see the pattern: the age spacing of the children in my family was fairly consistent. After my brother Ed's birth in 1937, the rest followed like Catholic clockwork. But after my sister Peg was born in 1943, there was a six-year gap before I arrived in January 1949. I suspect I was a Holiday Surprise. After graduating from college in 1970, I served the next four years in the U.S. Marine Corps. In 1971, I married **LEIGH A. ALOGNA** of West Haven, CT; in 1976, I embarked on a 26 year career with the FBI, retiring in New York in 2001. We currently split the year with residences in Florida and Connecticut. We have no children.

PART 2

THE MACKINNON CLAN

COMING TO NORTH AMERICA

B Y THE END OF THE AMERICAN REVOLUTION in 1783, the poor economic situation in the Scottish Highlands saw several tenants abandoning their land and emigrating to North America. In 1802, 400 Highland settlers landed in Sydney, Nova Scotia (NS), which was the first direct voyage of emigrants from Scotland to Cape Breton. Almost all of these early settlers were Gaelic speaking (Gaels) and were a complete mix of Roman Catholics and Presbyterians. In 1772, a wave of Gaels began to arrive in Prince Edward Island and in 1773, the ship *The Hector* brought 200 Gaels to Pictou, NS, thus beginning a new stream of Highland emigration, heralding the town's slogan as "The Birthplace of New Scotland."

The *Hector* settlers in Pictou had been Presbyterian. From that time, Catholic immigrants arriving in this port were often encouraged, by fellow Catholics, to join larger concentrations of Catholics in

Antigonish County or to move further east to Cape Breton where there was a relatively equal split of Catholic and Presbyterian Highland Scots. The town of Antigonish is where the McKinnon Clan settled in the New World.

Early accounts indicate that the family emigrated from the Isle of Eigg, Scotland, in the late eighteenth century. Eigg is one of the "Small Isles" in the Scottish Inner Hebrides island chain on Scotland's west coast. Situated just south of the Isle of Skye, it is a small island covering an area of some 12 square miles and loosely associated with the Scottish Highlands. The Isle offers little geographic or historical significance and to this day is populated by no more than a hundred Scots who call it home.

One would be remiss, however, not to mention the Isle of Eigg without reference to the famous "Eigg Massacre," a tale that has been passed down through generations. Wikipedia describes a sordid chapter between the MacDonalds and MacLeods, which was apparently similar to the infamous family feud between the Hatfields and McCoys:

> In 1577, according to Clan Ranald tradition, a group of MacLeods were being hosted on Eigg, when they became over-amorous towards local women. As a result, the local men (primarily the MacDonald clan) rounded the MacLeods up, and cast them adrift in the Minch (body of water), until they were rescued by MacLeods from elsewhere. Wanting revenge, a group of MacLeods landed on Eigg, but had been spotted by the islanders, who decided to hide in an obscure

cave called the Cave of Frances, located on the south coast; the entrance to the cave is tiny, and was obscured by moss, undergrowth, and a small waterfall.

The traditions go on to say that the MacLeods conducted a thorough but fruitless search for the inhabitants, but after 3–5 days, just as the MacLeods were leaving, they saw someone leave the cave, and were able to follow their footprints to the entrance. The MacLeods re-directed the water, piled thatch and roof timbers at the cave entrance, and set fire to it. Water dampened the flames, so that the cave was filled with smoke, asphyxiating all the MacDonalds inside, estimated to be some 400. Only one inhabitant of Eigg survived, an old woman, who had not sought refuge in the cave.

Serious doubt remains about the veracity of the tale. In fact, in later times, a minister of Eigg stated: "*The less I enquired into its history . . . the more I was likely to feel I knew something about it.*" Nonetheless, human remains in the cave have been reported over the centuries, though most of the remains have since been removed and buried elsewhere, and natural disturbances in the soil occasionally uncover further remains.

There are a variety of reasons for the emigration of Scots to the new world in the eighteenth century, most notably the *Highland Clearances* and the ever-increasing strife that existed between England and Scotland.

First, during the eighteenth and nineteenth centuries, a significant number of tenants were evicted from the Scottish Highlands through what was known at the time as the *Highland Clearances.* As the economy of raising sheep overtook farming, aristocratic landowners soon started a movement to evict farming families who were living in a given area such as an entire glen. The Clearances relied on the insecurity of most tenants' tenure under the Scottish legal system and resulted in large-scale voluntary emigrations over the same period from the area to the Scottish Lowlands, and further to North America and Australia. It was felt that these emigrations denigrated the cultural landscape of Scotland and destroyed much of their Gaelic culture.

Second, many of the Highland chieftains never took kindly to the union of England and Scotland. In 1715 and 1745, many clans, led by their chieftains, rose in rebellion for the purpose of restoring their ancient monarchs (namely the Stuarts) to the throne of Scotland. The Catholics of Scotland were devoted to the Stuart family because they considered that family justly entitled to the throne of Great Britain. But English soldiers under the command of the Duke of Cumberland took possession of the Highlands at various commanding points for the purpose of suppressing the rebellious clans. It is estimated that between 1763 and 1787, no less than 50,000 Scots left the Highlands, and of those, some 30,000 fled to North America. Catholic oppression, which prevailed in all Western Isles of Scotland in the 1770s, served to show the people that their only recourse lay in emigration.

As legend typically follows fact, other tales were passed down through generations to highlight the plight of the Catholics. One such tale was the "Religion of the Yellow Stick." An old version suggests that a priest from Coll (one of the Scottish Inner Hebrides Islands) was accustomed to driving "recalcitrant natives" to church by a smart application of his walking stick. Another version states that the stick's handler was none other than Hector, the son of Lachlan MacLean of Coll. He was the Laird (lord) of Muck in 1715, which is one of the smallest islands of the Inner Hebrides.[9]

Dr. Samuel Johnson, on his famous journey round the Hebrides in 1775, encountered the following story:

> In Rum [*another small island of the Inner Hebrides*], there were fifty-eight families who continued *Papists* [*practicing the Catholic religion*] for some time after the Laird became a Protestant. Their adherence to their old religion was strengthened by the countenance of the Laird's sister, a zealous Romanist, till one Sunday, as they were going to Mass under the conduct of their patroness, MacLean met them on the way, gave one of them a blow on the head with a yellow stick, I suppose a cane, for which the *Erse* [*Scottish Gaelic language*] had no [*appropriate*] name, and drove them to the *kirk* [*Protestant Church of Scotland*], from which they have never since departed. Since the use of this

---

9   Taken from "Religion of the Yellow Stick," accessed online at Wikipedia.com.

method of conversion, the inhabitants of Eigg and Canna [*westernmost Inner Hebrides island*], who continue Papists, call the Protestantism of Rum, the Religion of the Yellow Stick.[10]

---

10 From "Religion of the Yellow Stick."

L ITTLE IS KNOWN of our "pioneer" **JOHN MACKINNON** in terms of occupation or immediate (sibling) family. But it should be obvious why he decided to leave his homeland in search of a better life. John was born in Eigg in 1776. Some family trees identify his parents as Neil Mor MacKinnon and Christy MacNeil, but questions exist as to the accuracy and authenticity of those trees. I should reiterate that the surname "Mc" is used interchangeably with "Mac."[11]

(*Note:* Several family trees exist for the John MacKinnon family in such sites as Ancestry.com and FamilySearch.com hosted by the Church of Latter Day Saints, some of which go back to the fifteenth century and beyond. However, pertinent inconsistencies were apparent in terms

---

11   Scottish historian Ewan J. Innes authored an essay depicted on ScottishHistory.com in 1998, which argues that the surname "Mc" is used interchangeably with "Mac." In fact, he maintains that "Mc" is an abbreviated form of "Mac" and both were used in this manner throughout 19th century Scottish and Irish migration.

of names of spouses, dates and places of death, etc. to the point where reliability was in question. As a result, that research was not used in this book.)

Since sheepherding and farming were prevalent on the Isle of Eigg at the time, it is presumed that John's parents made their living either as farmers or herders.

What is also known is that in 1791, Colonel Fraser of Edinburgh brought a colony of settlers from Eigg to Pictou, Nova Scotia (NS). Colonel Fraser was a Scottish military officer who was interested in promoting emigration to Nova Scotia (for a price), and promised a ship if he could muster 350 emigrants.

Among the emigrants on this trip were **JOHN MACKINNON** (age 15), Donald McKinnon, three families of MacEacherns, three families of MacIsaacs, a family of MacDonalds, Donald MacLeod from Cann, and Neil MacLeod. It is not known the relationship between John and Donald MacKinnon, whether they were brothers, cousins, uncle-nephew, etc. But with the exception of Donald MacKinnon, all these people went to Parrsboro, in Cumberland County, NS, where they took up farming near Minas Basin, some 125 miles to the west of the town of Antigonish.

It was there that John MacLeod, father of Monsignor MacLeod, married Mary McDonald. After a few years, the immigrants began to realize their mistake in not following their Catholic countrymen to the County of Antigonish. Their farms promised well, but the outlook for their children was not hopeful. The land around them was peopled with non-Catholics, and it soon became evident that without priest or church, the surrounding influence would in the end prove disastrous to their ancestral faith.

After some nine years, in approximately 1800, the MacKinnons and MacLeods gave up their farms and came in time to Antigonish to occupy leading positions in the Church and county government. Among their descendants were Archbishop MacKinnon, Monsignor McLeod, Reverends W.B. McLeod, Alexander McLeod, Stephen McKinnon (a Trappist monk), the Honorable J. MacKinnon, his son J.J. McKinnon, and the Honorable James McLeod.[12]

Two years after he landed in Nova Scotia, **JOHN MACKINNON** married his childhood sweetheart, **EUNICE MACLEOD**, who also grew up on the Isle of Eigg. Eunice, who also went by "Una," was just 18 when they exchanged vows. During the course of the next 27 years, John and Una would settle in Antigonish and bear eight (8) children: 6 boys and 2 girls:

1. **Neil MacKinnon**, b. 1793.

2. **Lauchlin MacKinnon**, b. 1801.

3. **Ewan MacKinnon**, b. 1806.

4. **JOHN L. MACKINNON**, b. 1808.

5. **Colin Francis MacKinnon**, b. 1810.

---

12 Raymond A. MacLean, Ph.D., *History of Antigonish, Vol. 1* (Antigonish, NS: Casket Printing & Publishing Co., 1976).

6.   **Mary MacKinnon**, b. 1812.

7.   **Flora Catherine MacKinnon**, b. 1816.

8.   **Angus MacKinnon**, b. 1820.

1. **Neil MacKinnon**—John and Una's oldest child, Neil was born in Parrsboro, NS, in 1793 and later became a teacher. Although we know that he married **Sarah MacDonald** around 1815 and had three children, little else is known of Neil or Sarah other than the fact he died in North Grant, NS, in 1888 at the age of 95.

Little is known about Neil's siblings except for my great-great-grandfather **JOHN L. MACKINNON** and his brother **Bishop Colin F. MacKinnon**. Nonetheless, the following is what is known.

2. **Lauchlin MacKinnon**—Born in Pembroke, NS, in 1801, Lauchlin married **Ann MacDonald** around 1840 and the couple had four children. At the time of their marriage, Ann was 33 and Lauchlin, 39. Ann grew up in the Antigonish area and remained there until her death in 1869. Lauchlin passed away in 1875 at the age of 74. It is believed that he was a farmer by trade.

3. **Ewan MacKinnon**—Records indicate that Ewan was born in 1806 at the MacKinnon homestead in Williams Point, which is a section of Antigonish. At some point, he married **Mary MacDonald**, a young lady from Pictou, NS, just 50 miles west of Antigonish. Pictou is a port on the

north shore of NS, which was the main receiving point for many Scottish immigrants during the eighteenth century.

4. **JOHN L. MACKINNON**—My great-great-grandfather, "Honorable John" was born at Williams Point in 1808 and married **JEANNET CHISHOLM** in 1834. Jeannet's family was from North River, Antigonish. The couple had six children.

5. **Colin F. MacKinnon**—Born in 1810 at the family homestead in Williams Point, "Bishop" MacKinnon went on to develop a remarkable career in the Catholic Church. He died in 1879 at the age of 69 and is buried in a vault at St. Ninian's Cathedral in Antigonish.

John L. MacKinnon. Photo taken from a montage of the 1881 Legislative Council.

6. **Mary MacKinnon**—Also born at the family homestead in Williams Point (1812), Mary married **Laughlin MacDonald** and had fourteen (14) children: 9 boys and 5 girls. She passed in 1892 at the age of 80 in Clydesdale, NS.

7. **Flora MacKinnon**—Flora was born in 1816 at Williams Point, Antigonish. At some point, she married **Angus McVicar** and had nine (9) children. She was residing in Big Marsh, NS, when she died in 1886 at the age of 70. It is interesting to note that Flora's grandson, **Alexander**

McVicar, fought in South Africa's Boer War and was killed in action in 1900.

8. **Angus MacKinnon**—As the youngest son, Angus was born at Williams Point, Antigonish, in 1820. Records indicate that he married **Margaret MacIsaac** (born 1830) and was residing in Mahoney's Beach near Antigonish in 1891. A death certificate disclosed that they had at least one child (**Rebecca Chabot**) who died in 1904 of breast cancer in Brookline, MA.

THE THREE GIANTS

O F ALL THE ANCESTORS on the MacKinnon side of the family, the three that stand out based on their remarkable achievements and contributions to society are **Bishop Colin F. MacKinnon,** my grandfather **HUGH L. MCKINNON,** and my grandaunt **Sr. Genevieve Marie.** My grandfather will be addressed later in this chapter, and my grandaunt at the beginning of "The Locke Family" chapter.

Bishop Colin F. MacKinnon

Colin Francis MacKinnon was born on July 20, 1810 at Williams Point, in the village of Antigonish. The first school that Colin and his brother John attended was taught by their older brother, Neil MacKinnon, in North Grant, Sydney, Nova Scotia. In 1817, Neil had received a license issued by the Earl of Dalhousie, Lieutenant Governor of Nova Scotia, authorizing him to conduct school at Williams Point in the County of Sydney. In 1824, Colin attended the "classical" school instituted by his first cousin, Fr. William B. MacLeod, at Grand Narrows and later at East Bay, Cape Breton Island. Following this, he was sent to Rome by Bishop William Fraser, where he enrolled at the Urban College of the Propaganda in 1829. He received PhD and DD degrees and was ordained in Rome in 1837.

Bishop Colin MacKinnon, circa 1855.

Fr. MacKinnon was appointed a parish priest at St. Andrew's Parish in Sydney County, NS, where he remained for the next fifteen (15) years before his consecration as Bishop of Arichat by Bishop Walsh of Halifax, NS, in 1852. Arichat is one of the oldest communities in NS and is located approximately 60 miles east of Antigonish.

In 1838, he founded the renowned St. Andrew's Grammar School, which is similar to a present-day junior college with strong classical emphasis. Its future graduates would be numerous and impressive. They included a future bishop, more than a score of priests, a knighted

chief justice, a justice of the
Supreme Court of Nova
Scotia, a county court judge,
a dozen lawyers, members of
Parliament and the Provincial
Legislature, several doctors,
university professors, and a
legion of school teachers.
St. Andrew's soon became
"the place to go" for political,
religious, or educational
advancement in Nova Scotia.

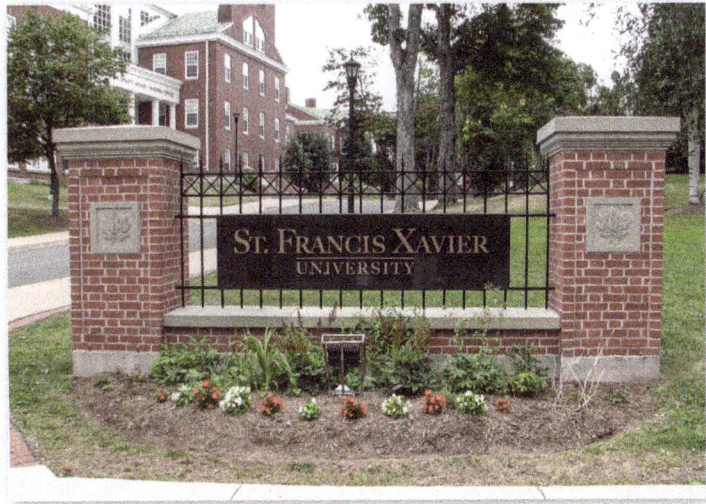

St. Francis Xavier University.

Furthermore, he established the Arichat Seminary in 1853, which
became St. Francis Xavier's College when it was moved to Antigonish
in 1855. St. Francis is currently one of Canada's top five universities. As
if that weren't enough, in the following year (1856), the Congregation
de Notre-Dame accepted his invitation to open the Arichat Convent;
and in 1860, the Brothers of the Christian Schools were engaged to staff
the Arichat Academy.

His greatest material undertaking was the building of the new stone
church in Antigonish, which would become the future St. Ninian's
Cathedral. Its planning and construction extended from October 1865,
when the Bishop announced his dream to the parishioners, until its
completion and opening in September 1874.

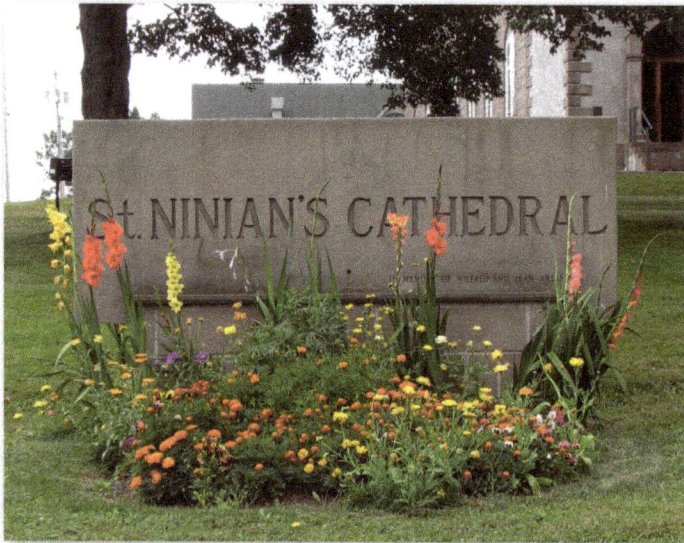

St. Ninian's Cathedral, the Roman Catholic Seat for the Diocese of Antigonish, located on the campus of St. Francis Xavier University.

Bishop MacKinnon resigned in 1877 and was succeeded by Bishop John R. Cameron, Coadjutor Bishop of Arichat. Bishop MacKinnon died on September 26, 1879 and was buried in the vault beneath the high altar of St. Ninian's Cathedral, despite the fact that his tomb is located at the St. Ninian's Cemetery.

The tomb of Bishop MacKinnon at St. Ninian's Cemetery.

In addition, a cairn[13] was erected in his honor adjacent to the old MacKinnon house at Williams Point.

Statue of Bishop MacKinnon statue as it stands today on the campus of St. Francis Xavier University.

The cairn dedicated to Bishop MacKinnon adjacent to the old MacKinnon house.

13 Known as the Cairn at Williams Point, this memorial commemorates the birthplace of Bishop Colin F. MacKinnon and was dedicated on September 25, 2005. "Cairn" is a Scottish Gaelic term for a man-made stone mound.

"Honorable" John L. MacKinnon

My "grandfather's grandfather" was **JOHN L. MACKINNON**. Nicknamed "Honorable John," he was born in 1808 at the Williams Point homestead in Antigonish.

Although a farmer by trade, "Honorable John" was a "self-made man," and despite his limited education, he soon entered the world of politics. He was elected along with his good friend, W. A. Henry, to the Nova Scotia Legislative House of Assembly, representing Sydney County for a four-year term in 1851. Both he and Henry were subsequently re-elected three more times in 1855, 1859, and 1863. In 1863, however, the county was split, at which time Antigonish became a separate constituency with **JOHN L. MACKINNON** and W.A. Henry representing it until 1867.

JOHN began his political career with the Reform Party but switched to the Liberal-Conservative Party in 1857 over the issue of Joseph Howe's quarrel with the Irish Catholics of Halifax.[14] One of the ten men who crossed the floor to join the Conservative opposition to defeat the Reform (Liberal) government in 1857, **JOHN** was also a member of the Executive Council from 1863 until 1867. After his defeat in 1867 over

---

14 In 1854, William Young was elected premier of the Nova Scotia House of Assembly. His government was accused of overlooking Catholics, and tensions with Catholics were exacerbated by Provincial Secretary Joseph Howe's rupture with Nova Scotia's Irish Catholic community over his recruitment of Americans to fight on the British side in the Crimean War. In February 1857, ten Catholic and two Protestant liberals voted with the Tories to bring down Young's government.

a Confederation issue,[15] **JOHN L. MACKINNON** became a member of the Legislative Council where he remained until his death in 1892. He also held the position of agricultural commissioner during that time.

In 1834, **JOHN L. MACKINNON** married **JEANNET CHISHOLM**, a young lady from North River, Antigonish County. During the next eleven years, **JEANNET** would give birth to the following six children:

1. **Margaret MacKinnon**, b. 1835.

2. **Mary MacKinnon**, b. 1838.

3. **Catherine MacKinnon**, b. 1841.

4. **Eunice MacKinnon**, b. 1846.

5. **Alice MacKinnon**, b. unknown.

6. **JOHN J. MACKINNON**, b. 1847.

1. **Margaret MacKinnon**—Born at Williams Point, Antigonish in 1835, Margaret married **William Grant** in approximately 1855, and subsequently had nine (9) children. She died in 1869, some twenty-two years before her husband William passed in 1891. All of their children remained in Nova Scotia except for one son, **William "Willie" Peter Grant** who married **Mary MacKinnon** from Cape Breton (different

---

15 The Canadian Confederation was a process by which the British colonies of Canada, Nova Scotia, and New Brunswick were united into one Dominion of Canada on July 1, 1867.

William "Willie" Peter Grant, a nephew of great-grandfather John J. MacKinnon.

family) and moved to California to become chief of the Caledonian Society of Berkeley, CA.[16] Willie was still residing in Berkeley when he passed away in 1947.

2. **Mary MacKinnon**—Also born at Williams Point, Mary married **Angus MacIsaac** in 1855. Angus was from the Hallowell Grant neighborhood of Antigonish. Nicknamed "The Tailor," he was a harness maker by trade. They had two children, **John Angus MacIsaac** who was a banker, and his brother, **William Bernard MacIsaac**. Mary died in 1867 at the age of 39.

3. **Catherine MacKinnon**—In 1866, Catherine exchanged vows with **Andrew MacFarlane** at the Antigonish Catholic Church. A year later, Catherine gave birth to her first son, **Colin Francis MacFarlane**, at Williams Point, Antigonish. Colin would be blessed with a sister, **Mary**, two years later in 1869, but Mary would never reach her 14th birthday, as she passed in 1882. Colin's brother **John** met a similar fate as he died in 1882, shortly after his 10th birthday. The youngest of Catherine's sons, **Ronald Andrew MacFarlane**, was born in 1876. After some twenty

---

16 Founded in the early nineteenth century, the Caledonian Society of Berkeley eventually merged with the Society of San Francisco (founded in 1866) and is one of the oldest societies in California that promotes Scottish culture and traditions.

years with Canada's Intercolonial Railway, Ronald retired as a section foreman. He passed away in 1927 at the age of 51.

4. **Eunice MacKinnon—Hugh Cameron** married his childhood sweetheart, Eunice, in 1865. Over the next twenty years, Eunice would bear eleven (11) children, three of which would not survive their adolescent years. Of the remaining eight children, three would move to Montreal and one to Halifax, NS. Eunice passed away in 1910 at the age of 64. Her husband, Hugh, survived eight more years and was buried in Cape Breton, NS, in 1918.

5. **Alice MacKinnon**—No information was available regarding Alice.

6. **JOHN J. MACKINNON**—My *great-grandfather*, **JOHN J. MACKINNON**, was born at the family homestead at Williams Point on July 29, 1847. He was the only son of the "Honorable" **JOHN L. MACKINNON. JOHN J. MACKINNON** became a professor at St. Francis Xavier's College (as it was known early on); he later studied law in Halifax and became assistant clerk in the House of Assembly. He married **CHRISTINA MACDONALD** in 1874, the daughter of **PROFESSOR RODERICK ("RORY DENOON") MACDONALD**, pioneer and longtime professor at the college and first Inspector of Schools

John J. MacKinnon, circa 1875.

for Antigonish and Guysborough counties. **John J. MacKinnon** was a barrister (attorney) by trade and represented Antigonish County in the Legislative Assembly from 1874 to 1877. Sometime after his resignation, he moved to Manitoba Province in central Canada, presumably in pursuit of employment opportunities.

In late 1883, calamity struck the MacKinnon family. **CHRISTINA MACKINNON** died unexpectedly in Antigonish on October 20, 1883 at the age of 29, leaving five children all under the age of ten. If that wasn't enough, three months later, **JOHN J. MACKINNON** passed away at 34 years of age on January 10, 1884. He is buried in Winnipeg, Manitoba Province, where he had been residing at the time. The cause of death of either parent has never been definitely determined.

One unsubstantiated account of **JOHN**'s passing was that he was shot to death following a card game dispute in Thunder Bay, Ontario, which was then part of the Northwest Territory. More intriguing is the fact that Thunder Bay is almost 400 miles from his home in Winnipeg, a considerable distance to travel in the day. **JOHN**'s obituary, however, places him in Ontario Province at the time of his death.

J.J. MacKinnon obituary.

Death of J. J. McKinnon.

In October last we chronicled the early and universally regretted death of Mrs J. J. McKinnon. To-day we have to note a kindred event, which is if possible a sadder still the untimely death, far away from home and friends, of that lamented lady's husband. On Thursday last, John I. McKinnon Jr. formerly a Barrister of Antigonish, and son of Hon. John McKinnon M. L. C., died at Prince Arthurs Landing, N. W. T., A little over a year ago he left here in the bloom of health and strength; and the news of his death at the early age of 36, threw a gloom over our community where he was so well and favorably known. He was one of the most genial and open-hearted of men; those who differed from him recognized his fine personal qualities His immediate connections find his death a hard blow, and they have our heart-felt sympathy in their bereavement.

Nonetheless, during their first seven years of marriage, John J. and Christina had five (5) children:

1. **John George MacKinnon**, b. 1874.

2. **Colin F. MacKinnon**, b. 1875.

3. **Roderick MacKinnon**, b. 1877.

4. **HUGH L. MCKINNON**, b. 1878.

5. **Janet ("Jennie") MacKinnon**, b. 1881.

1. **John George MacKinnon**—The oldest boy, "George," was born in Antigonish on January 18, 1874. According to the 1921 Canadian Census, George was an engineer by trade when he married his wife, **Henrietta** (maiden name McKinnon). They had one child, **Roderick**, and moved at some point to Nanaimo, British Columbia (near Vancouver). George died in 1962 at the age of 87.

2. **Colin F. MacKinnon**—Colin was born in 1875 at Williams Point, Antigonish and earned his living as a coal miner. He married **Sarah McDonald** and had three children: **Colin** (b. 1894), **Isabella** (b. 1898), and **Margaret May** (b. 1900). He passed away in Cape Breton in 1909 at the age of 34.

3. **Roderick MacKinnon**—Roderick was born in Antigonish on February 3, 1877. He appeared to follow his older brother George's

footsteps in moving to the west coast of Canada. From there he traveled extensively throughout Asia. In 1924, at the age of 47, a ship's manifest confirmed that he returned home to Vancouver after spending some time in Shanghai. Four years later, in 1928, he arrived in Saint John, New Brunswick from Antwerp, Belgium. Roderick never married and died in Vancouver in 1960 at the age of 83.

4. HUGH LAUGHLIN MCKINNON—My grandfather Hugh was born at Williams Point, Antigonish on April 21, 1878. As the **second** *"giant"* of the MacKinnon family and the youngest son of **JOHN J. MACKINNON**, details on his life follow in the next section.

5. Janet ("Jennie") C. MacKinnon—"Aunt Jennie" was the youngest of the five siblings. It is unclear exactly when she was born. Records in Nova Scotia record the year of her birth as 1879 and place of birth as Antigonish, NS However, when she died in 1952 in Dorchester, MA, she was laid to rest at the family gravesite in Milton, MA, which indicates 1881 as her year of birth. The 1920 census seems to suggest that she was living as a boarder with the Spires family on Ashmont St. in Dorchester. At that time, she was employed at a chocolate mill as a "candy packager," possibly at the old Walter Baker facility at the Lower Mills in Dorchester. Not much else is known about Aunt Jennie other than she may have suffered some emotional problems later in life.

Hugh Laughlin McKinnon

The second "*giant*" of the MacKinnon family and youngest son of my great-grandfather **JOHN J. MACKINNON** was my grandfather **HUGH LAUGHLIN MCKINNON**. Born at Williams Point, Antigonish on April 21, 1878 and orphaned at the age of 5, **HUGH** immigrated to Boston in 1893 at the age of 15 and, in 1902, petitioned for naturalization.[17] Despite his limited education (fifth grade), Hugh learned and excelled at anything he set his mind to do. He was the proverbial "self-made" man.

In 1907, while living at 122 Park St. in Dorchester, **HUGH** married **ANNE B. LOCKE** who was the oldest of five children. Her father, **EDWARD LOCKE**, was an Irish immigrant who lived at 242 Neponset Ave. with his wife, **MARY G. DOLAN**. Hugh would eventually buy this two-story house across from St. Ann Catholic Church some ten years later and call it home for the next forty-one (41) years.

Baptismal Certificate
St. Ninian Cathedral Parish
P.O. Box 1628, Antigonish, NS   B2G 2L8

Issued: August 28, 2013

Name:	Hugh Laughlin McKinnon
Place of Birth:	Antigonish, NS
Date of Birth:	April 21, 1878
Date of Baptism:	April 29, 1878
Father:	John McKinnon
Mother:	Christina McKinnon
Sponsor:	Christopher McDonald
Sponsor:	Sarah McDonald
Clergyman:	Rev. Hugh Gillis
Confirmation:	N/A
Marriage:	N/A

I certify that this is a true copy taken from the Baptismal Register of the above Church.

Baptismal certificate for Hugh Laughlin McKinnon

---

17 His Baptismal Certificate, dated April 29, 1878, notes his given name as Hugh Laughlin McKinnon as attested by his parents, John MacKinnon and Christina MacKinnon. At some point after his naturalization, he changed his middle name from Laughlin to Lawrence. Further, Hugh maintained the "Mc" surname throughout his life as evidenced by the Canadian census for 1891; the US Census for 1910 and 1940, his WW II Draft Registration card, and his gravestone at the Milton Cemetery.

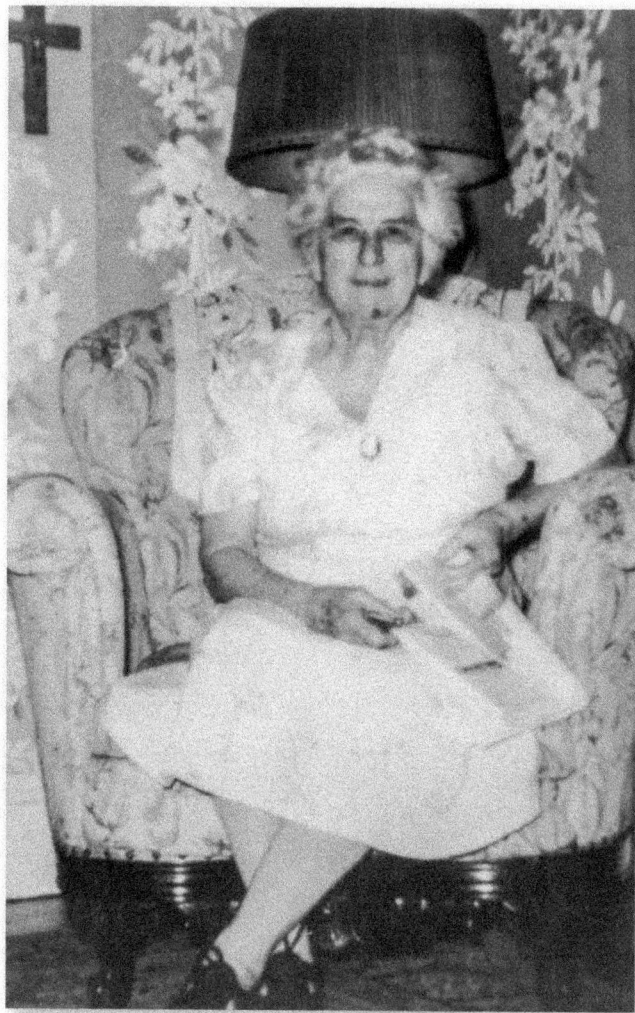

Anne B. Locke, circa 1948.

By 1910, **HUGH** was 28 and he and Anne had the first two of six children, namely my mother, **ALICE**, who was born in 1908, and my Aunt Mary who was born in 1910. By the time the First World War was declared in 1917, he had already secured a government job with the U.S. Navy. According to his military draft registration, which he completed in 1918, he was employed as a machinery inspector at the Victory Plant in Squantum, MA, a component of the U.S. Naval Air Station.[18] After the plant shut down in 1920, Hugh continued to work for the Navy for the next twenty-six years in various capacities and at various locations including the Boston Naval Shipyard and the Fore River Shipyard in Hingham, MA.

HUGH retired in 1946 from the Fore River Shipyard after fourteen years of service. During this time, his accomplishments at Fore River were recognized by the U.S. Navy as directly contributing to the shipyard's high scores in warship production and construction. His obituary in the Quincy *Patriot Ledger* credited **HUGH L. MCKINNON** with "earning two awards presented by the War Production Board for speeding Naval ship work by his inventive ability." One of these prestigious commendations,

---

18 Naval Air Station Squantum was an active naval aviation facility during 1917 and from 1923 to 1953. The original civilian airfield that preceded it, the Harvard Aviation Field, dates back to 1910. The base, which was sited on Squantum Point in the city of Quincy, MA, abutted Dorchester Bay, Quincy Bay, and the Neponset River. Used primarily as a seaplane base and flight training facility until 1917, the land was converted by the Navy to a shipyard called the Victory Destroyer Plant. Although owned by the Government, the facility was operated by Bethlehem Shipbuilding Corp. and was designed specifically to construct the *Clemson*-class destroyer. Thirty-five of these ships were built at this location before the plant was closed in 1920. The area is now utilized by Squantum Point Park, Boston Scientific Corp., and the condominium development, Marina Bay.

Hugh L. McKinnon receiving a U.S. Navy citation.

which was presented by two Navy admirals, had seldom been awarded to any civilian employee (there were only fourteen recipients nationwide). It credited **HUGH** for "his ingenuity in saving thousands of dollars for the government and speeding up production of essential parts." He also received a number of cash awards for production suggestions and was recommended for a salary increase by the Navy's Advisory Committee.

Fore River Navy Inspector Wins National Award

WPB Honor Goes To Hugh McKinnon For Production Ideas

National honors in naval ship construction were awarded yesterday afternoon on behalf of the War Production board, Washington, D.C., to Hugh L. McKinnon, Fore River navy inspector, who also won national honors in 1905 as amateur champion middleweight and welterweight boxer in the 145-pound class. Capt. H. F. D. Davis, USN, supervisor of shipbuilding here, presented the award for the WPB.

Machine Inspector

McKinnon is supervising machinery inspector for the Navy at the Fore River yard of piping fabrication that is tested to pressures as high as 15,000 pounds each square inch. He has worked there for 10 years and has been in the navy's service for 28 years at Fore River, the Boston Navy Yard, and the Victory plant, Squantum.

McKinnon's son, Hugh L. McKinnon, Jr., formerly an electric welder at Fore River and Lawley shipyards and now a first class shipfitter in the U. S. Navy, was cited last year for heroic action aboard the new light cruiser USS Montpelier, in battle against the Japs in the South Pacific.

McKinnon also received three cash awards for production suggestions and has been recommended for a salary increase by the Navy's local committee of which the chairman is Capt. M. G. Vangeli, USN, officer-in-charge at the Bethlehem-Hingham shipyard.

Award of national honors to Mc-

(Fore River)

Kinnon was made in Captain Davis' office at Fore River in the presence of the suggestion committee and shipbuilding leaders. Captain Davis commended McKinnon for having competed successfully in a navy-wide program that netted thousands of production suggestions.

Captain Davis reported that McKinnon's production suggestion was the only one awarded national honors to originate among supervisor of shipbuilding personnel. He added that it was personally pleasing to him to have such recognition come to a member of his force.

Ingenuity Praised

The citation read by Captain Davis in behalf of William F. Todd, chief of staff, War Production Board, said: "Today as never before American industry in its all-out war effort is relying on the man with ideas. The ingenuity and initiative shown in your suggestion leads us to hope that the board will have occasion to review other suggestions from you at its future meetings."

McKinnon lives at 242 Neponset avenue, Dorchester, is married, has seven children and 10 grandchildren. He has another son, Seaman 1/c Joseph McKinnon of the navy, who formerly worked at the Hingham shipyard.

McKinnon's major suggestion was for a burr remover for use inside pipes. He also suggested use of an adjustable glass for interior views of pipes, and a chain pipe cleaner for removal of scale, sand and dirt from inside pipes.

Capt. William H. Magruder, USN, assistant to Captain Davis, participated in the award and congratulated McKinnon for having speeded the war effort to higher production.

Captain Vangeli said that McKinnon was one of 34 winners who earned national honors in the latest navy-wide schedule as part of a progressive movement aimed at the development of creative action by workers in a management labor program.

In attendance at the award were members of the navy's suggestion committee: Graydon Abbott, supervising naval architect, Fore River; Miss Claire Demarest, recorder of the committee and secretary to Captain Vangeli; Philip Sheehan, chief warship inspector at Lawley's yard; G. C. Tucker, supervising machinery inspector, Hingham shipyard; P. J. Collins, chief warship inspector, Fore River; H. A Hope, principal marine engineer, Fore River, and Paul Crosby, supervising electrical inspector, Fore River.

Others present were Lt. E. A. Pilkington, USN, assistant machinery inspection officer at Fore River; Angus D. MacDonnell, president, Society of American Shipbuilders and Designers, and James A. Vincent, supervising machinery inspector, Fore River.

From the Quincy Patriot Ledger, c. 1946.

In addition to his professional accomplishments, **HUGH L. MCKINNON** was described by a columnist for the *Dorchester Beacon* (a Boston newspaper) this way:

Hugh L. McKinnon as a boxer. circa 1905.

Hughie was one of the greatest all around athletes ever known in these parts and in 1905 was the National Welterweight Boxing Championship in San Francisco, [and] the year following he won the heavyweight as well as the welterweight (*boxing*) championship in Chicago. In *football*, he played for the old Dorchester Associates; and in later years, coached the old Neponset Wanderers; in *baseball*, he starred for many years with the old St. Vincent's Holy Name Society; and in *swimming*, had no peer either for endurance in cold weather at swimming or in long distance and year after year was one of the familiar persons on the beach when Tenean (beach) was in its infancy.

M'KINNON THE STAR OF AMATEUR BOXERS

AMATEUR CHAMPIONS OF 1905

105-pound Class—Fred Stingel, Boston.

115-pound Class—Sam Moss, Waltham.

125-pound Class—Willie Cornell, Lowell.

135-pound Class—A. J. McGarry, New York.

145-pound Class—H. L. McKinnon, Dorchester.

158-pound Class—Jack Egan, Bryn Mawr, Penn.

Heavyweight Class—Emory Payne, New York.

Jiu jitsu, buck and wing movements, knockout wallops, and blows that never reached home figured in the amateur championship sparring contests at Mechanics' Hall last night, for science had taken to the woods, and contortionists and sprinters had the floor, while between 3500 and 4000 amused spectators cheered and laughed themselves hoarse over the volleys of blank cartridges that the ambitious pugs fired at one another, two score and 10 hopeful scrappers perforated the atmosphere somewhere between the cellar and the ceiling with windmill swings, while the referees danced nimbly about the ring to escape being knocked out themselves.

Police Captain Made a Champion

Incidentally Captain Donovan of Station 16 had the honor of making a champion last night, for when Jack Egan of Bryn Mawr, Penn., who had beaten Mayer of New York in the 158-pound class, lined up against H. McKinnon of Dorchester in the 145-pound category, the latter made so little of the difference in weight and was handing it so vigorously to the Pennsylvania boy in the third round, that the doughty captain stuck his billy up and certified to Egan's ability to dispose of his man.

It was a night of many mills and there was fun galore. There were foul football tackles where both scrappers lost their balance, their wind and their tempers; there were championships lost by chance blows; there were all kinds of reaches, attitudes and crouches, and there was laughter always.

One of the amusing incidents was contributed involuntarily by a New Yorker who plied the towel for Mayer, last year's Olympic champion at St. Louis. At the end of Mayer's first round with Egan of Philadelphia, the former's second, in a voice plainly audible 100 feet away, censured his principal for "showing sympathy." All the sympathy there was needed right at home, however, as the New Yorker was handily disposed of by Egan in the third round.

Only one of the championships went to the New York entries, and this was in the 135-pound class, where McGarry of New York, in the third round of the finals, defeated Randolph of South Boston, who had already won his two pre-

Perhaps the greatest surprise of the night was the showing in the 145-pound class of McKinnon of Dorchester, for after giving the quietus to Prowse of New York in the very first round, he clearly outpointed the clever Egan, who had previously won out over Mayer in the 158-pound class.

Plucky Gus Lenny of South Boston after winning three preliminaries in the 115-pound class, went down to defeat before Sam Moss of Waltham. Though Moss was undoubtedly fully as clever as Lenny the latter's three previous bouts evidently accounted for his poor showing in the final.

Two South Boston midgets met in the finals of the 105-pound class, but Fred Stingel, who is evidently in a class by himself, won the championship inside of one round.

One of the cleverest bouts of the night was presented in the second mill of the 135-pounders, where Al Britt of the Boston Y. M. C. A., who fought his way to the semi-finals in the 125-pound class last year, lost to E. E. Randolph in the first mill that he entered.

The funniest feature of the bouts was contributed by a fighter named Fox, with a reach like Fitzsimmons and a crouch like Jimmy Briggs. But the crouch and the attitude proved his undoing.

The judges were Eugene Denny of the B. A. A. and Dr. J. J. Flynn of the C. G. A.; referees, Frank Peters and Neil Doherty, B. A. A., and timekeeper, Hugh McGrath.

The summaries:

105-POUND CLASS.

(Trial Bouts.)

John J. Conroy, Delphi A. A., beat Bud Fredericks, Everett, three rounds.

Fred Stingel, South Boston, beat Joe McKee, Boston, two rounds.

(Final Bout.)

Fred Stingel beat John J. Conroy, one round.

115-POUND CLASS.

(Trial Bouts.)

Sam Moss, Waltham, beat J. S. Kelly, Medford, one round.

Smith, Mott Haven A. C., New York, beat C. Hoyt, Chelsea, two rounds.

Gus Lenny, Franklin A. A., Boston, beat Fox, Boston, two rounds.

H. Schlumbohm, Mott Haven A. C., New York, beat Bernard J. Diamond, Independent A. A., Brooklyn, three rounds.

(First Semi-finals.)

Gus Lenny beat Smith, two rounds.

Sam Moss beat K. McCarthy, Nashua (bye), three rounds.

(Second Semi-finals.)

Gus Lenny beat H. Schlumbohm, three rounds.

(Final Bout.)

Sam Moss beat Gus Lenny, three rounds.

125-POUND CLASS.

(Trial Bouts.)

Willie Cornell, Lowell, beat Drew, Everett, one round.

J. A. Sullivan, Independent A. A., Brooklyn, beat J. F. Sullivan, Boston, three rounds.

(Semi-final Bout.)

Willie Cornell beat T. F. Fitzpatrick, Tiger A. A., South Boston (bye), three rounds.

(Final Bout.)

Willie Cornell beat J. A. Sullivan, three rounds.

135-POUND CLASS.

(Trial Bouts.)

Undated Boston newspaper, c. 1905.

Medals won by Hugh L. McKinnon for competition in the high jump.

More of **HUGH**'s credits include his membership with the Fore River Naval Associates, St. Anne's Holy Name Society, and the Massachusetts Catholic Order of Foresters. Above all, however, **HUGH MCKINNON**'s priority was always his family. Nothing was more important to him than spending time with his children and grandchildren. He died at home on June 4, 1948 after a long illness. He was 70 years of age and is buried at the Milton Cemetery.

Quincy Ledger

Obituaries

Funeral Is Held For Retired Fore River Shipyard Inspector

The funeral for Hugh L. Mac-Kinnon, 70, retired U. S. Navy engineering inspector of Fore River shipyard and in 1906 the national amateur champion light middleweight boxer of the United States, was held Monday from his home, 242 Neponset avenue, Dorchester, followed by a solemn high requiem mass celebrated in St. Anne's church, Dorchester. Burial was in Milton cemetery.

Mr. MacKinnon died Friday in his home after a year's illness. Two years ago he retired at Fore River after 14 years' service there, during which he aided the yard score highest records in warship construction. He earned two awards made by the War Production board for speeding Naval shipwork by his inventive ability.

Before joining Fore River he was employed for 21 years at the Boston Naval shipyard as a production marine engineer on ship construction and repair. Before his Navy duty he was in private marine employ on the South Shore.

He was a native of Antigonish, N. S., and came to the United States when he was 11. As an athlete he excelled in many sports and in later life was an L street Brownie, devoted to swimming through the year. Highlight of his sports career was winning the AAU light middleweight boxing crown in San Francisco, Cal.

Mr. MacKinnon was a member of the Fore River Naval associates, St. Anne's Holy Name society and the Massachusetts Catholic order of Foresters.

Cong. John W. McCormack of Boston, minority floor leader, attended the pre-burial rites. The Navy at Fore River was represented at the funeral by James Vincent, chief engineering inspector; Albert J. Reinhalter, George V. Haley, Angus D. MacDonnell and George O. E. Nelson.

Survivors include his wife, Mrs. Anne (Lock) MacKinnon; two sons, Hugh L. MacKinnon, Jr., and Joseph MacKinnon of Dorchester; four daughters, Mrs. Alice Duff of Milton, Mrs. Mary Rothengast of New York, Mrs. Anne O'Neil of Dorchester and Mrs. Ruth Lunny of New Haven, Conn.; a sister, Miss Jennie MacKinnon of Dorchester, and 11 grandchildren.

MCKINNON RITES AT ST. ANN'S CHURCH

The funeral of Hugh L. McKinnon, 70, of 242 Neponset Ave., was held from his home Monday morning followed by a Solemn High Mass of Requiem at 9:00 at St. Ann's Church, celebrated by Rev. Fr. Francis J. Dinan, assisted by Rev. Fr. John J. Geegan, deacon and Rev. Fr. Edward J. Splaine as sub-deacon.

Mr. McKinnon was born in Nova Scotia and came to Fields Corner at the age of 12 and had lived in Dorchester and Neponset the past 58 years. 'Hughie' was one of the geratest all round athletes ever known in these parts and in 1905 was the National Welterweight Boxing Champion in San Francisco, the year following he won the heavyweight as well as the welterweight championship in Chicago. In football he played for the old Dorchester Associates and in later years coached the old Neponset Wanderers; in baseball he starred for many years with the old St. Vincent's Holy Name Society and in swimming had no peer either for endurance in cold weather at swimming or in long distance and year after year was one of the familiar persons on the beach when Tenean was in its infancy. Many persons today can thank Hughie for his friendly interest and patience in teaching them to swim and many a mother could relax on the beach when he was around, knowing that their offsprings would never be allowed to venture out too far.

He was employed as a Senior Inspector in the Navy Yard and during World War I was stationed at Squantum, World War II he was at Fore River and was the proud possessor of a Commendation by two Admirals of the Navy from the War Production Board which were only given out to 14 in the entire country. This certificate was for his ingenuity in saving thousands of dollars for the government and speeding up production of essential parts.

He was a member of St. Ann's Holy Name Society and St. Peter's M.C.O.F. and is survived by his wife, Mrs. Ann Locke McKinnon, two sons, Hugh Jr. of Dorchester a Boston fireman attached to Ladder 17 and Joseph of Dorchester, 4 daughters, Mrs. John F. O'Neil of Dorchester, Mrs. Edward Duff of Milton, Mrs. John F. Lunney of New Haven, Conn. and Mrs. William Rothengast of New York, and a sister Miss Jennie McKinnon and 11 grandchildren.

Burial was at Milton Cemetery with Rev. Fr. John J. Geegan saying the committal prayers.

From the Quincy Patriot Ledger, June 1948.

THE LOCKE FAMILY

THE OLDEST OF FIVE, my grandmother **ANNE B. LOCKE** was born in Boston on November 25, 1882 to **EDWARD** and **MARY G. (DOLAN) LOCKE**. As of 1900, **EDWARD** (1854–1914), who described his trade as "nail maker," had emigrated from County Leitrim in Ireland. His wife, **MARY**, was a local girl, born in Chelsea, Massachusetts, just outside of Boston.

Aunt Molly / Sr. Genevieve Marie

As mentioned earlier, there were three notable figures on my mother's side of the family. The third *"giant"* of the McKinnon/Locke family was my grandmother's sister, **Mary C. Locke**, who was born in Dorchester on October 14, 1884. An extremely bright lady and strong achiever, she was nicknamed "Molly" at an early age. She soon realized she had a vocation for religious life and proceeded to achieve her academic and professional goals.

After obtaining a bachelor's degree from Boston College, Mary went on to Catholic University in Washington, D.C. where she received a master's degree in education. At the completion of her studies, she assumed her final religious vows and entered the order of St. Joseph as Sr. Genevieve Marie. Nonetheless, she was always "Aunt Molly" to us. During her extensive career, she assumed a variety of high-level positions at various academic institutions. From 1932 to 1941, she was president and Sister Superior at Regis College, a renowned women's

Sr. Genevieve Marie, previously Mary C. Locke, circa 1965.

college in Weston, MA, and was among one of its first presidents. From this position, she went on to be supervisor of the Sacred Heart School and convent in Newton Center and community supervisor for the Congregation of the Sisters of St. Joseph. In 1965, she returned to St. Agatha's in Milton, MA, as a "senior sister," a quasi-retirement position, and she remained in residence at St. Agatha's convent for many years. However, in the twilight of her career, she was named Sister Superior at the Holy Name Convent in West Roxbury and Assistant Mother of her order, namely, the Congregation of the Sisters of St. Joseph (C.S.J.).

After an illustrious career, she passed away on May 2, 1970 at the Bethany Convent in Framingham, MA, after a brief illness. Sr. Genevieve Marie was 86 years of age and was laid to rest at St. Patrick's Cemetery in Natick, MA.

Gravestone of Sr. Genevieve Marie, aka "Aunt Molly."

Aunt Bess

The third Locke sister was **Elizabeth D. Locke**, born February 12, 1887, five years after my grandmother. "Aunt Bess," as she was commonly known to my immediate family, was somewhat of a mysterious character. Although she lived in our town of Milton, I don't recall seeing very much of her when I was living at home. In fact, she was somewhat shunned and avoided by my immediate family except, of course, by my mother. Although she was perceived to be quite wealthy, Aunt Bess was not particularly friendly and uncharacteristically frugal, especially with her relatives. But that sense of frugality did not extend to the church. She appeared to be closer to her sister Mary (Aunt Molly) than to her other siblings, a relationship that fostered financial generosity with the Sisters of St. Joseph.

Whenever Aunt Bess paid an unexpected visit to our house in Milton in her big, dark green Chrysler, it was somewhat daunting, if not intimidating. As kids, we closed the doors and pulled the shades. Peering through a small window that we used to determine if we were home or not, we would watch as she meandered up the front walk and knocked on the door. Answering that door, however, was not an option. And despite her relative "still youthful" age, she was not an attractive woman, and bore a striking resemblance to Eleanor Roosevelt. Need more be said!

However, if my mother was home, there was always a different outcome. Aunt Bess would be greeted with open arms. My mother had a heart of gold and the "gift of gab."[19] She would talk to anyone at any time, and Bess was no exception. She would be warmly welcomed with a cup of tea and engaging conversation. For my mother, no topic was too trivial.

Bess could be described as an "old maid." She never married and worked her entire life. As youngsters, we had been told she had a good job at the phone company and saved most of what she earned, making her a very *rich old maid*. Looking back, it's unfortunate that she was avoided by most of our family based on her reputation to be both unfriendly and cheap, which was questionable, if not unfounded. But one day, sweet revenge would be hers!

What we do know about Aunt Bess is that in 1900 when she was still in school, she was living at 44 Tolman St. in Dorchester with her parents and four siblings. Ten years later, her family had moved a short distance away in Dorchester to Neponset Ave. After graduating from high school, Bess worked as a weaver in a textile mill in the Boston area. When her father died in 1914, Bess moved with her mother to Fairview St. in Dorchester where she lived with her two aunts. For the next few years, she worked as a secretary for a cleaning business, and then, by the late 1920s, she was hired as a stenographer for the Suffolk County Court House, certainly a good job at the time. Apparently, she saved much and invested well. By early 1931, she had saved enough money to purchase—and move into—her father's old house on Tolman Street. Quite an accomplishment for a single woman of her age.

---

19 An old Irish expression referring to anyone who can speak well and eloquently. The "gift" is received by kissing the Blarney Stone in Ireland.

International (tourist) travel in those days was limited to the very affluent, especially during the years of the Great Depression (1929–1939). As air transportation did not become popular for another twenty years, steamship travel was the norm. It was also unusual for a woman to travel alone as it was expensive and offered an array of security risks. However, those concerns didn't deter Aunt Bess. Starting in 1930 when she was just 43, Aunt Bess began a life of international travel that would span the next twenty-five years. Not only did she visit the Canadian Maritime Provinces (regularly), but her journeys took her to Italy, Germany, France, Great Britain, and Argentina. Her trip to Germany in 1938 was particularly daring in light of Hitler's seizure of Austria and the start of his military expansion throughout Europe. Nonetheless, her cruising continued for the next fifteen years on such prestigious ships as the White Star liner *Britannic* and the renowned *Queen Elizabeth* on its return voyage from France to New York in 1950. By the mid-1950s, immigration records indicate that she flew to a variety of new destinations such as Hawaii and Mexico.

In 1956, she moved from Dorchester to School Street in Milton. Although Bess was close to both of her sisters, as noted earlier, it appears she was closer to Aunt Molly and her religious community, the Sisters of St. Joseph, and she maintained that relationship throughout her entire life. While a resident of Milton, Bess outlived all of her siblings and died in Milton on September 7, 1977 at the age of 90. She is buried at Mt. Calvary Cemetery in Mattapan (Boston) along with her parents.

What is interesting about Bess is that she apparently acquired a considerable amount of wealth during her lifetime. Although she never worked for the phone company as her family had presumed, she did well in the stock market and specifically in AT&T stock. The home that her estate sold upon her death was worth over $1 million in today's dollars.

As her family would soon learn, Aunt Bess was as fastidious about her finances in death as she was during her life. Although all of her relatives (e.g., nieces, nephews, grandnieces, etc.) eagerly awaited results of her will and distribution of her assets, they soon realized that Bess's *entire estate* was bequeathed to a series of religious charitable entities, such as the *Propagation of the Faith, Jesuit Missions,* and the *Society of African Missions, Inc.* Not one dime went to a relative. For Aunt Bess, revenge was sweet indeed!

Elizabeth "Aunt Bessie" D. Locke's gravestone.

The Commonwealth of Massachusetts

OUT-OF-TOWN   **BOSTON**

1 PLACE OF DEATH

SUFFOLK
(County)

BOSTON
(City or Town)

SECRETARY OF THE COMMONWEALTH
DIVISION OF VITAL STATISTICS

**STANDARD
CERTIFICATE OF DEATH**

(City or Town making this return

1977

Registered No. 06650

No. H 2003 CARNEY HOSPITAL   St. {If death occurred in a hospital or institution, give its NAME instead of street and number}
PHYSICIAN—IMPORTANT

2 FULL NAME   ELIZABETH D. LOCKE
(If deceased is a married, widowed or divorced woman, give also maiden name.)

{If deceased a U. S. War Veteran, specify WAR} no

(a) Permanent Residence, No. 166 SCHOOL   St. MILTON, MA 02186
(City or town and State)

MEDICAL CERTIFICATE OF DEATH	PERSONAL AND STATISTICAL PARTICULARS

3 DATE OF DEATH SEPTEMBER 07 1977
(Month) (Day) (Year)

9 SEX	10 COLOR	11 SINGLE (write the word) MARRIED WIDOWED DIVORCED UNKNOWN
F	W	Single

4 I HEREBY CERTIFY that I attended deceased from
SEPT. 02 19 77 to SEPT. 07 19 77
I last saw h ER alive on SEPT 07 19 77 death is said to
have occurred on the date stated above, at 2:15AM m.

12 If married, widowed, or divorced
HUSBAND of ....
(Give maiden name of wife in full)
(or) WIFE of ....
(Husband's name in full)

DEATH WAS CAUSED BY: IMMEDIATE CAUSE | INTERVAL BETWEEN ONSET AND DEATH

(a) PULMONARY EMBOLI

Due To
(b)

Due To
(c)

13 AGE 90 Years Months Days | If under 24 hours Hours Minut

14 Usual Occupation Clerk
(Kind of work done during most of working life)

OTHER SIGNIFICANT CONDITIONS FRACTURE RIGHT HIP

15 Industry or Business Suffolk Cty- Registry of deeds

Was autopsy performed? No
What test confirmed diagnosis? CLINICAL

16 Social Security No. 025-36-5894

17 BIRTHPLACE (City) (State or country) Boston, Mass.

5 Was disease or injury in any way related to occupation of deceased? No
If so, specify

18 NAME OF FATHER Edward Locke

19 BIRTHPLACE OF FATHER (City) (State or country) Boston Mass.

(Signature) Arthur E. Sullivan M.D.
ARTHUR SULLIVAN M.D.
(Print or Type Name)
(Address) CARNEY HOSPITAL Date SEPT 07 19 77

20 MAIDEN NAME OF MOTHER Mary Dolan

21 BIRTHPLACE OF MOTHER (City) (State or country) Boston Mass.

6 Mt Calvary   Boston, Mass.
Place of Burial or Cremation   (City or Town)
DATE OF BURIAL September 10, 1977 19

22 I HEREBY CERTIFY that a satisfactory standard certificate of deat
was filed with me BEFORE the burial or transit permit was issued:
R. Maynie L 21160
(Signature of Agent Board of Health or other)
Sept. 7, 1977

7 NAME OF FUNERAL DIRECTOR W. Craig Dolan
ADDRESS 1140 Washington St. Dorchester, Mass.

(Official Designation)   (Date of Issue of Permit)
Received and filed SEP 12 1977   19

8 INFORMANT Sister Mary Beatrix CSJ
(Address) 444 Centre St. Milton, Mass.
02186

William J. Kane
A True Copy Attest: (Clerk or Registr

Witness my hand and the Seal of the Town of Milton

this 22nd . day of Aug . 20 16 .

Susan M. Galvin

TOWN CLERK

Elizabeth Locke's death certificate.

Edward and Charles

The two Locke brothers that were known to us in the early years were **Edward L. Locke** and **Charles J. Locke**.[20]

Edward L. Locke (1889–1944) married **Marion E. McLaughlin** (1893–1980) and had three children: **Edward L. Locke Jr.** (1916–1971), **Rita M. Locke** (1918–1992), and **Evelyn F. Locke** (1922–2010). Edward senior was a crane operator at the Navy Yard in Boston.

The second brother, Charles J. Locke (1895–1954), married **Helen Agnes Evans** (1892–1958) and had two children: **Edward P. Locke** (1925–1997) and **Thomas L. Locke** (1926–1988). "Cousin Tommy," who lived in Milton, was very close to my mother and visited her on a regular basis. Tom's father, Charles, worked for Bethlehem Steel at Fore River during WWII and made a living as a lather[21] and painter in Weymouth, MA, in later years.

---

20 Further research has determined, however, that my grandmother (Anne B. Locke) may have had several other siblings not previously identified. Dr. Edward L. Locke, the 6th (b. 1972) has done a considerable amount of research on the Locke family including travelling to Ireland. He resides in Auburn, AL and is the grandson of Edward L. Locke (1889–1944). His research indicates that there were four other siblings: Alice Locke (1892–1894), Joseph Locke (1891–1891), Rita Locke (dates unknown), and Evelyn Locke (dates unknown).

21 A lathe is a device used to shape metal, wood, and pottery.

(Aunt) Mary and Alice McKinnon (Mom) in 1914

B Y THE TIME the United States entered the First World War, my grandparents **HUGH** and **ANNE MCKINNON** raised six (6) children:

1. **ALICE MCKINNON**, b. 1908.

2. **Mary G. McKinnon**, b. 1910.

3. **Anna McKinnon**, b. 1912.

4. **John J. McKinnon**, b. 1913.

5. **Ruth Mae McKinnon**, b. 1915.

6. **Hugh E. McKinnon**, b. 1917.

7. **Joseph M. McKinnon**, b. 1926.

1. ALICE MCKINNON—As the oldest of many children and, later, the mother of a half dozen more (the first of whom was born less than a year after she was married), my mother, **ALICE**, must have had little time to herself. (See more on my mother in Part 1 under **EDWARD "EDDY" DUFF**, and later in this section about the "Mac Sisters.")

2. **Mary G. McKinnon**—My aunt Mary was born in 1910; she married **William A. Rothengast** in 1938. "Uncle Bill," who was a true gentleman, had been a detective with the New York City Police Department (NYPD) in the Bronx since 1936. Both of Bill's older brothers had also joined the NYPD in various capacities.

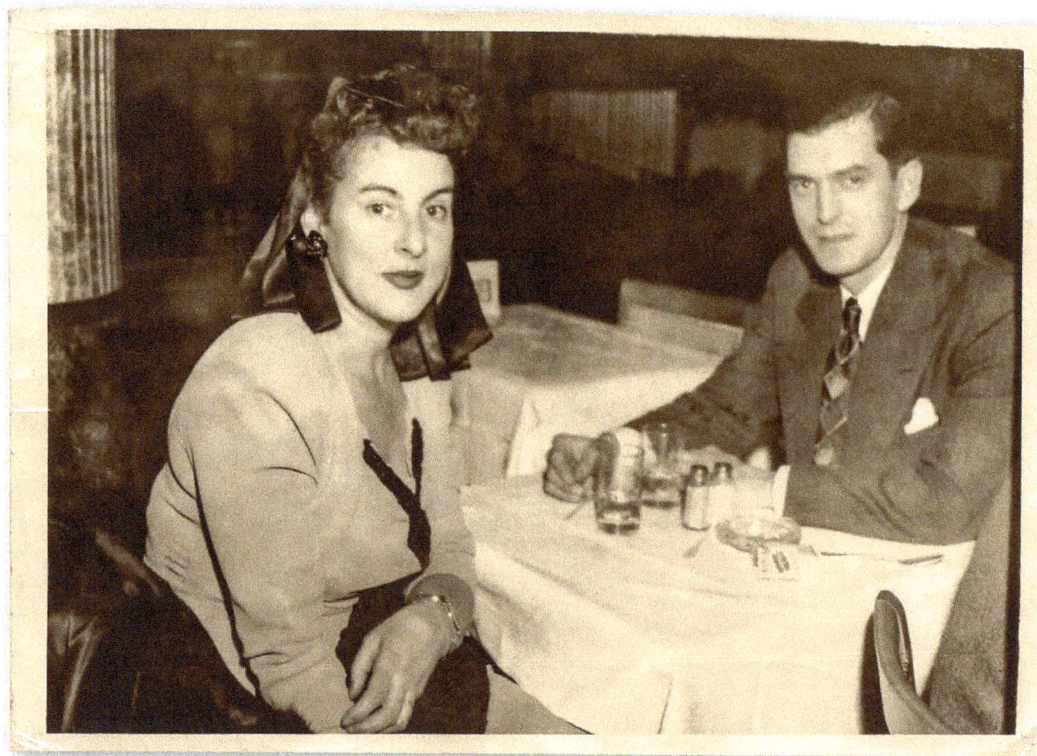

Mary and Bill Rothengast in New York City, 1939.

Bill's oldest brother, Conrad H. Rothengast (born 1898), had joined the force in 1921. He rose through the ranks to ultimately become a chief inspector with the NYPD. Conrad retired in 1953 to Manhasset, NY, where he remained until his death in 1963, just eight months after his younger brother—my uncle Bill—passed away. The middle brother, Joseph Rothengast (born 1900), had joined the department in 1925 as a patrolman. He retired in 1956 and moved to Ft. Lauderdale, Florida, with his family; he passed away in 1989.

Having no children, Bill and Mary lived in the Bronx until Bill retired. During that time, Mary pursued a career in nursing and attained her certification as a registered nurse. After Bill's retirement, they moved to South Florida and lived in a variety of communities that included Pompano Beach and Ft. Lauderdale. Bill worked as a salesman for Sears while Mary was employed as a nurse at Holy Cross Hospital in Ft. Lauderdale. When Bill passed away in 1963, Mary moved back to Dorchester, MA, and continued to work in private nursing. She died five years later in 1968 and is buried at New Calvary Cemetery in Mattapan, Massachusetts.

Gravestone for my aunt Mary Rothengast.

3. **Anna B. McKinnon**—Anna was my mother's second sister, born under the Aquarius sign on Saturday January 27, 1912. At the time, her parents and sisters were living at 242 Neponset Ave. in Dorchester. After high school, Anna took a job with Western Union as a telegraph operator, which was considered a very good job in its day. Nonetheless, she left Western Union and was soon working for a dentist in Dorchester as a dental assistant. Dr. Joseph Daily maintained his practice for many years and eventually became our family dentist.

Anna was an independent sort and wasn't in any hurry to settle down. However, she soon met the "love of her life," and in 1937, she married **John Francis O'Neill** (born 1911), also of Dorchester. "Uncle John" was a "jack of all trades" and a very talented man. He held a variety of positions before and during the war that included machinist, electrician, and engineer. But if Uncle John had a passion, it was bowling. He was most likely one of the top-rated amateur candlepin bowlers in Boston at the time.[22] I recall my father taking us kids to the Lucky Strike Bowling Alley in Dorchester on Friday nights to watch Uncle John perform. He consistently made a small fortune hustling would-be "marks," who naively underestimated his ability. His official "day job," however, was as a "boiler room" engineer, which included working on heating systems in commercial buildings and in some cases, breweries. One such brewery

---

22 Candlepin bowling is a variation of bowling that is played primarily in the Canadian Maritime Provinces and the New England states. It was developed in 1880 in Worcester, MA, by Justin White, a local bowling center owner, some years before the standardization of the ten-pin bowling sport in 1895 and the invention of duckpin bowling. The balls are considerably smaller than those used in duckpin bowling.

he worked at was the old Star Brewery on Shirley Street in Roxbury.[23] Both he and his brother Dan O'Neill were members of the International Union of Operating Engineers.

Anna and John had three children: **John Jr.** (**"Jack"**), **Ann Marie**, and **Danielle**. Aunt Anna passed away in 1968 at the age of 56. Uncle John died almost twenty years later in 1987 at 76 years of age.

Gravestone of Anna and John O'Neill.

---

23 Star Brewing Co. opened in 1933 and closed in 1952, spanning some nineteen years. The brewery was active during Prohibition, which makes it an oddity. Some breweries were able to stay in business by producing "near-beer" which had very little alcohol. Others switched over to bottling sodas or other beverages and some even became ice houses or other related businesses. At the time Star Brewery was operating, Boston was considered an "active brewing" city boasting some forty-eight breweries— significantly more than any other comparably sized city.

4. **John Joseph McKinnon**—Back in the day, it was uncommon for births to occur at the local hospital. Instead, mothers typically gave birth at home. My grandmother's first son, John Joseph McKinnon, was born on March 5, 1913 in Dorchester, at the address listed on his birth certificate as the residence of **HUGH L. MCKINNON** and **ANNE B. (LOCKE) MCKINNON**. Not much is known about John, other than at the time of his death in 1933, he was living with my grandparents on Neponset Ave. He had been working as a laborer for a steamship company in Boston for two years. He died in an automobile accident on Randolph Ave. in Milton. It was rumored that when the accident occurred, John was dating a girl from Randolph and was "hitch-hiking" a ride from Dorchester to see his sweetheart for the proverbial Saturday night date. Although the driver of that vehicle survived that horrendous accident, unfortunately John did not. He was only 20 years old. John is buried in the Duff/McKinnon family plot at the Milton Cemetery.

Grandfather Hugh's sister Jennie with John McKinnon.

The Commonwealth of Massachusetts

DEPARTMENT OF PUBLIC HEALTH
REGISTRY OF VITAL RECORDS AND STATISTICS

R 0061027

The Commonwealth of Massachusetts
OFFICE OF THE SECRETARY
DIVISION OF VITAL STATISTICS
**MEDICAL EXAMINER'S
CERTIFICATE OF DEATH**

Milton
(City or town making return)

430

PLACE OF DEATH	
Norfolk (County)	Milton (City or Town)
No. Milton Hospital St., Ward	Registered No. 85~

(If death occurred in a hospital or institution, give its NAME instead of street and number)

2 FULL NAME John J. McKinnon
(If deceased is a married, widowed or divorced woman, give also maiden name.)

(If U.S. War Veteran, specify WAR)

(a) Residence. No. 242 Neponset Ave. St., Ward, Neponset
(Usual place of abode)   (If nonresident, give city or town and state)

Length of residence in city or town where death occurred yrs. mos. days. How long in U. S., if of foreign birth? yrs. mos. days.

PERSONAL AND STATISTICAL PARTICULARS

3 SEX	4 COLOR OR RACE	5 SINGLE MARRIED WIDOWED or DIVORCED (write the word)
Male	White	single

5a. If married, widowed, or divorced
HUSBAND of _____ (Give maiden name of wife in full)
(or) WIFE of _____ (Husband's name in full)

6 IF STILLBORN, enter that fact here.

7 AGE 20 Years ___ Months ___ Days ___ If less than 1 day Hours ___ Minutes ___

OCCUPATION
8 Trade, profession, or particular kind of work done, as spinner, sawyer, bookkeeper, etc. Laborer 7899
9 Industry or business in which work was done, as silk mill, saw mill, bank, etc. Steamship Co.
10 Date deceased last worked at this occupation (month and year) May 27, 1931
11 Total time (years) spent in this occupation 2 yr

12 BIRTHPLACE (City) Neponset
(State or country) Mass. 30

PARENTS
13 NAME OF FATHER Hugh McKinnon
14 BIRTHPLACE OF FATHER (City) Nova Scotia 10-6
(State or country)
15 MAIDEN NAME OF MOTHER Annie Locke
16 BIRTHPLACE OF MOTHER (City) Boston, Mass. 30
(State or country)

17 Informant (Address) Hugh McKinnon 242 Neponset Ave. Neponset

I HEREBY CERTIFY that a satisfactory standard certificate of death was filed with me BEFORE the burial or transit permit was issued:
G. Frank Kemp
(Signature of Agent of Board of Health or Clerk)
Town Clerk May 30, 1933
(Official Designation)   (Date of Issue of Permit)

MEDICAL CERTIFICATE OF DEATH

18 DATE OF DEATH May 28, 1933
(Month) (Day) (Year)

19 I HEREBY CERTIFY that I have investigated the death of the person above-named and that the CAUSE and MANNER thereof are as follows: (If an injury was involved, state fully)

Hemorrhage
Crush of chest and abdomen
Multiple lacerations

2.10 m
(See reverse side for description for unknown person)

20 If death was due to external causes (VIOLENCE) fill in the following:
Accident, Suicide or Homicide? _____ Date of Injury May 28, 1933

Where did Injury occur? Milton Mass.
(City or town and State)

Manner of Injury Crushed by an auto
Nature of Injury Collision

21 Was disease or injury in any way related to occupation of deceased? _____
If so, specify _____
(Signed) Fred E. Jones M.D.
(Address) Quincy, Mass. Date 5/31/33

22 PLACE OF BURIAL, CREMATION OR REMOVAL Calvary (Cemetery) Boston (City or town)
DATE OF BURIAL May 31, 1933 19

23 NAME OF UNDERTAKER Joseph A. Farrell
ADDRESS 256 Adams St. Dorchester

Received and filed May 30, 1933 19

A TRUE COPY, ATTEST: G. Frank Kemp (Registrar)

OCT 11 2013

Gerald J. Kyle
Registrar of Vital Records and Statistics

I, the above-signed, hereby certify that I am the Registrar of Vital Records and Statistics; that as such I have custody of the records of birth, marriage, and death required by law to kept in my office; and I do hereby certify that the above is a true copy from said records.

Death certificate of John McKinnon.

5. Ruth Marie McKinnon—The youngest daughter of **HUGH AND ANNE MCKINNON**, "Aunt Ruthie" was born in Dorchester on March 14, 1915. She was the last component of the four "Mac Sisters" as they would forever be known. To say these sisters were close was an understatement. To use the old adage, they were "as thick as thieves," intensely loyal to each other, and formidable opponents if one were to be so unwise as to take issue with one or all.

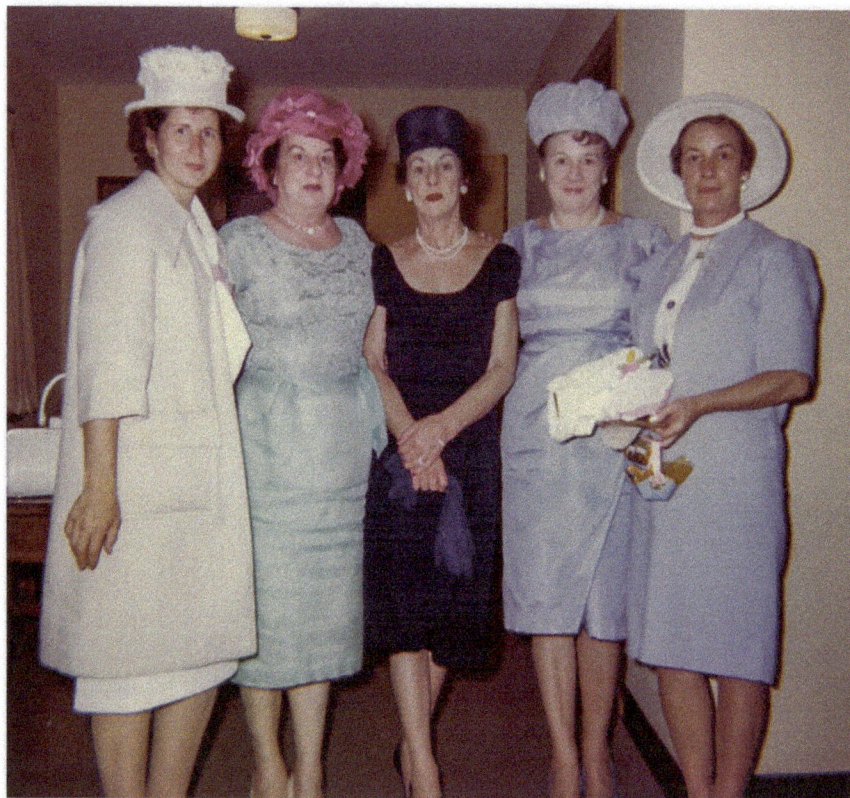

Shown here (in 1963) at far left is my aunt Mary (Jencyowski) MacKinnon (her husband was my uncle Hugh MacKinnon, the only sibling to spell his last name with a "Mac") with the four Mac Sisters, left to right: Anna (McKinnon) O'Neill, Mary (McKinnon) Rothengast, Alice (McKinnon) Duff, and Ruth (McKinnon) Lunny.

As mentioned earlier, the Mac Sisters' father, **HUGH L. MCKINNON**, was an "all around" athlete. Needless to say, he encouraged his children to compete athletically as well. Swimming was a somewhat popular activity due to the proximity of nearby beaches in Dorchester and South Boston. All of the "Mac Sisters" were good swimmers and a few competed in local swim meets. In an undated article, the *Boston Globe* printed the following account under the caption "M'Kinnon Sisters Take Away Honors":

> The McKinnon sisters, Mary and Ruth Mae, representing Tenean Beach (Dorchester), scored 19 of the possible 36 points in the girls' events yesterday in the final championship swimming meet conducted by the Park Department at the Head House, South Boston. Mary McKinnon won both the 100-yard free-style and the 440-yard swim. Ruth Mae won the 50-yard (swim) and finished second in the 440 yard (swim), and finished third in the 100-yard breast stroke.

On September 11, 1937—a date that decades later would be characterized by tragic events (2001)—two of the Mac sisters, Ruth and Anna, celebrated a festive double wedding at St. Anne's Church in Neponset with hundreds of relatives and friends. Their sister "Miss" Mary McKinnon acted as maid of honor for both.

On that day, Ruth shared vows with **John Francis Lunny** (b. 1910), an engineer with the West Haven, CT, School Department. According to the

The double wedding of Ruth and Anna McKinnon, September 11, 1937.

1930 census, Uncle John had lived on Willow Wood Street in Boston and worked as an electrician with Western Electric at Boston's South Railroad Station. He then took a similar job at New Haven's Union Station in CT. Both his father, James Joseph Lunny (a Boston firefighter) and his mother, Alice Anastasia O'Brien, were born in Boston. After Ruth's wedding in 1937, the young couple moved to Milford, CT, until the Second World War broke out in 1941. When, in 1942, John enlisted in the U.S. Navy as an electrician, Ruth moved back with her parents to Neponset Ave. in Dorchester. During the war, John participated in the invasions of North Africa, France, and Italy, where he was wounded and awarded the Purple Heart. A decorated hero, he also was awarded the Bronze Star for "Bravery Under Fire" in Tunisia; and a second Bronze Star for meritorious actions taken during the invasion of Sicily in July

1943. During the final months of the war, he was sent to the Far East, Indochina, and India before his discharge in September 1945.

The Lunnys had three children: **James**, **John**, and **Ruth**. Uncle John Lunny passed away in 1975 at the age of 65; and Aunt Ruthie in 1985 at the age of 70. Both are buried at All Saints Cemetery in North Haven, Connecticut.

6. **Hugh Edward MacKinnon**—1917 saw the birth of **HUGH** and **ANNE**'s second son and youngest child, Hugh Edward MacKinnon[24]. With flaming red hair and an engaging personality, he was soon known to friends as "Red" MacKinnon. Taking after his father, young Hugh soon learned electric welding at the Fore River Shipyard and worked there as a journeyman. He later worked in a similar position at Lawley's Yard[25] in Neponset. His hobby, however, was firefighting, and he volunteered on several occasions with the Quincy Fire Department.

When the Second World War was declared in 1941, Hugh was still working as a welder and living with his parents at 242 Neponset Ave. in Dorchester. But like many of his friends and relatives, he chose to enlist

---

24 Although not conclusive, sources indicate that Uncle Hugh's mother (Anne Locke) attempted unsuccessfully to convince his father, Hugh McKinnon (b. 1878) to change to the traditional "Mac" spelling. After his father died in 1948, Hugh's mother again raised the issue with young Hugh who was receptive and acceded to his mother's request prior to his marriage in 1951.

25 George Lawley & Son was a shipbuilding firm operating in Massachusetts from 1866 to 1945. It began in Scituate, then moved to Boston. After founder George Lawley (1823–1915) retired in 1890, his son, grandson and great-grandson upheld the business, which continued until 1945. Of the hundreds of ships built by the Lawleys, highlights include the yachts *Puritan* and *Mayflower*, respective winners of the 1885 and 1886 America's Cup.

1947

A motley crew: Uncle Hugh MacKinnon, Dad, and good friend Louie Jacobs.

in the military service. In 1942, Hugh joined the U.S. Navy and was sent to the Pacific where he would remain until his discharge in 1945. During that time, he was commended by the Navy for "courageous performance in the line of duty for actions taken in the Southwest Pacific Ocean."

Following the war, he moved back in with his parents and took a full-time position with the Boston Fire Department's Ladder 17 near Meeting House Hill in Dorchester.

In 1951, Hugh married **Mary Delores Jencyowski**, a 21-year-old Lithuanian girl from East Cambridge, MA. Mary was born to Frank and Bessie Jencyowski on May 20, 1930. She attended Thorndike Elementary School in Cambridge, and continued on to Cambridge High School where, in her senior year, she had to quit school to care for her ailing mother who suffered from breast cancer until her death at age 48. Shortly thereafter, Mary met Hugh and courted until their marriage in 1950. Within a few years, they moved to Centre Street in Dorchester where their three children were born: **Frances Ann**, **Ann Bernadette**, and young **Hugh**.

On August 15, 1961, my uncle Hugh would succumb to fire-related injuries, which he incurred in the line of duty. In 1964, Mary bought her first house in Brockton, MA, where she raised their children. Years later, she sold that house, moved to West Palm Beach, FL, and worked at an elder care facility. In 2001, she moved back to MA to be closer to her family. Mary currently resides in a nursing home in Brockton, the same town where she had bought her first house some fifty-four years before. She is the last remaining relative of her generation.

Hugh is buried at New Calvary Cemetery in Mattapan, MA. Besides Mary, Hugh is survived by their three children, all of whom live in communities south of Boston.

Hugh MacKinnon with his parents Anne and Hugh McKinnon.

Gravestone of my uncle, Hugh E. MacKinnon.

Joe McKinnon, about 1949.

7. **Joseph M. McKinnon**—The last name etched on the back of the McKinnon-Duff gravestone is Joseph M. McKinnon, who we always called "Uncle Joe." He was born in Hartford, CT, on July 2, 1926, and lived with my grandparents on Neponset Ave. until high school, which he left when he was in the tenth grade. All accounts paint him as a handsome young man with a full head of dark, curly hair, reserved if not quiet. Photographs display an interest in boats and planes, symbolic of travel and adventure, not unlike most boys his age. It was also said that he had an interest in photography and wished to pursue a career as a professional photographer. But as a practical matter, he needed a job and found employment as a laborer at the Hingham Shipyard.

Another factor preempted Joe's dream of a career in photography. The world was consumed by conflict and his country was calling. There was a war going on and he felt an obligation to serve like his brother Hugh and many of his friends in the neighborhood. But Joe wouldn't turn 18 until 1944, and who knew how long the war would last. However, as luck would play out, the war in both theaters was going strong, and recruiters would not let age interfere with their need to fill weekly quotas.

Despite the fact that his brother Hugh and brother-in-law John Lunny were in the Navy, Joe wanted to be different. He had seen some of the young Marines home on leave for a few days right out of boot camp.

He loved their tailored uniforms and their *gung-ho* spirit. Joe McKinnon thought he wanted to become a Marine. Unfortunately, Joe's experience at Marine boot camp at Parris Island the summer of 1943 was not what he had expected. He didn't last very long, but still wanted to serve. He returned to Dorchester and in November 1943, after misstating his age again, he enlisted in the U.S. Navy. Following basic training, he was designated an electrician's helper with the rank of Apprentice Seaman.

Although he enlisted for two years, Joe didn't adapt well to the Navy's military regimen. Within a few months, he started leaving his post without authorization, described by the military as Absent Without Leave (AWOL). At first it was only for a few days, but soon he was chronically AWOL. As expected, the Navy had little tolerance for such conduct especially during wartime. At first there were fines and demotions, but as the transgressions grew worse, court marshals were convened and periods of incarceration ordered. Surprisingly, Joe was discharged in 1946 with an *honorable discharge* after serving less than three years. By then the war was over.

Strangely enough, Joe re-enlisted four months later—that time for four years! It's unclear whether he hadn't learned his lesson from the Navy, or if the Navy hadn't learned theirs. But the transgressions grew worse. It came as no surprise that in November 1947, a General Court Marshal found him guilty of desertion and a host of other serious violations. The sentence was severe: reduction in grade, eleven months' confinement, and a "Bad Conduct Discharge," which was the proverbial "kiss of death" for future employment endeavors.

Following his discharge in 1948, Joe returned to Dorchester only to have his father die within two months. Although the elder McKinnon had been sick for almost a year, the shock to Joe and his family was severe. He needed an escape, and since he had previously been stationed in Brooklyn, NY, he succumbed to the lure of New York City. At some point, he took a job as a laborer in New York with the Pennsylvania Railroad.

In 1953, some five years after his discharge, Joe requested a copy of his military record from the Navy Department, which was sent to his then residence, the Broadway Central Hotel on Broadway in Manhattan. (When it was originally built in 1870, the hotel was lauded as the largest hotel in the world.) On May 22, 1954 (sixteen months after his military record had arrived at the Broadway Central), Joe McKinnon died somewhat mysteriously at the age of 27. His death was unexpected; few details were known other than that he fell off a building and died of multiple fractures and shock.

More than a few theories surfaced surrounding Joe's untimely passing. However, all were discounted despite the fact that the medical examiner ruled out "natural causes, accident, suicide, and homicide." Regardless of who or what precipitated the fall, the sober reality is that he died a few weeks before his 28th birthday. On a larger scale, his passing was unremarkable. Sadly, he was most likely one of hundreds that died that day in New York City.[26]

---

26 A more comprehensive review of Joe McKinnon's life, titled "Uncle Joe," was prepared in 2016 and disseminated to his family.

Certificate of Death

Certificate No. 156-54-111246

FILED

MAR 15 5:07

1. NAME OF DECEASED *JOSEPH McKINNON*
(Print or Typewrite)   First Name   Middle Name   Last Name

PERSONAL PARTICULARS (To be filled in by Funeral Director)	MEDICAL CERTIFICATE OF DEATH (To be filled in by the Physician)

2 USUAL RESIDENCE: (a) State *Mass.*

(b) Co. _____ (c) Post Office and Zone *Dorchester*

(d) No. *242 Neponset* Ave. (If in rural area give location)

(e) Length of residence or stay in City of New York immediately prior to death *N.R.*

3 SINGLE, MARRIED, WIDOWED, OR DIVORCED (write the word) *Single*

4 DATE OF BIRTH OF DECEDENT (Month) *July* (Day) *2* (Year) *1926*

5 AGE *27* yrs. ___ under 1 year mos. ___ days ___ If LESS than 1 day hrs. or ___ min. ___

a. Usual Occupation (Kind of work done during most of working life, even if retired) *Laborer*

b. Kind of Business or Industry in which this work was done *Penn. R.R.*

7 SOCIAL SECURITY NO. _____

8 BIRTHPLACE (State or Foreign Country) *Mass.*

9 OF WHAT COUNTRY WAS DECEASED A CITIZEN AT TIME OF DEATH? *U.S.A.*

10a. WAS DECEASED EVER IN UNITED STATES ARMED FORCES? *Yes*   10b. IF YES, Give war or dates of service *WWII*

11 NAME OF FATHER OF DECEDENT *Hugh McKinnon*

12 MAIDEN NAME OF MOTHER OF DECEDENT *Annie Roche*

13 NAME OF INFORMANT *Mary Rothengast*   RELATIONSHIP TO DECEASED *Sister*   ADDRESS *3321 Bruckner Blvd. Bronx*

14a. Name of Cemetery or Crematory *Milton Cemetery*   14b. Location (City, Town or County and State) *Milton Conn.*   14c. Date of Burial or Cremation *May 29 1954*

21 FUNERAL DIRECTOR *Metropolitan Funeral Service Co.*   ADDRESS *718 Second Av.*   PERMIT NUMBER *2800*

15 PLACE OF DEATH: (a) NEW YORK CITY: (b) Borough *MANHATTAN*

(c) Name of Hospital or Institution *BELLEVUE* (If not in hospital or institution, give street and number.)

(d) If elsewhere than in hospital or own residence, specify character of place of death, as hotel, office, store, street, taxicab, etc. *HOSPITAL*

16 DATE AND HOUR OF DEATH (Month) *MAY-* (Day) *22* (Year) *1954* (Hour) *A. M.*

17 SEX *MALE*   18 COLOR OR RACE *WHITE*   19 Approximate Age *27 yrs*

20 I HEREBY CERTIFY that, in accordance with the provisions of law, I took charge of the dead body at *CITY MORTUARY* this *23* day of *MAY* 19*54*

I further certify from the investigation and (complete autopsy) (partial autopsy) (incision) (examination) that, in my opinion, death occurred on the date and at the hour stated above and resulted from (natural causes) (accident) (suicide) (homicide) (undetermined circumstances pending further investigation), and that the causes of death were:

PART I

(a) Immediate Cause *MULTIPLE FRACTURES.*

(b) and (c) Antecedent Causes with Primary Cause Stated Last. due to (b) *SHOCK.* due to (c)

PART II

Contributory Causes

Signed _____ Assistant Medical Examiner

M. E. Case No. *4087*   *Milton Helpern, M.D.* Chief Medical Examiner   *5-1-54*

BUREAU OF RECORDS AND STATISTICS   DEPARTMENT OF HEALTH   CITY OF NEW YORK

DATE ISSUED   JAN 7, 2000.   DOCUMENT NO. *D 711301*

VR134-22CM-3 98 M818044

Joseph McKinnon's death certificate.

CONCLUSION

THE JOURNEY for this family research was insightful, fun, and, yes, sometimes frustrating! Best of all, it was worth it to have unearthed the pieces of the past and assembled them in a way that I hope honors them all. They are part of us—and we are part of them. And like good neighbors, I am happy to now "know" them.

Speaking of neighbors, it is interesting that both my parents lived a good portion of their pre-marriage lives as neighbors next door to each other—that my father's family lived at one address while my mother's family lived literally steps away. Was it a coincidence that, like several of their ancestors, they were neighbors? Their homes were across the street from St. Ann Catholic Church, school, and rectory—in an era when the church was typically the core of the community and the neighborhood. Both of my grandmothers were deeply religious; their close proximity to St. Ann's had a lasting impact on the lives of both women and on their children's upbringings.

240 & 242 Neponset Ave., Dorchester, MA.

Although the McKinnons originated from Scotland, there were distinct immigration similarities with their neighbors, the Duffs. The number of Irish immigrants who came to Newfoundland gradually grew from around 1,000 persons per year in the 1730s to some 5,000 a year in the late 1770s, when the total summer population swelled to around 30,000. By that time, the Irish comprised more than two-thirds of the total annual population of Newfoundland from the British Isles. Similarly, at the end of the eighteenth century, there was a mass migration from Scotland to the Canadian Maritime Provinces, most notably to Nova Scotia.

What I found most impressive was the courage and stamina these new immigrants displayed in risking everything they had for a better life in the new world. That determination was certainly highlighted by my family pioneers Arthur Duff and John MacKinnon as they displayed an incredible drive to do what their parents and grandparents feared could not be done. This in and of itself made me appreciate what they accomplished.

And though discovering the "facts" and their stories had been my primary goal, I had not anticipated that this project would also give me the opportunity to meet new friends and relatives and connect with others whom I had not seen in many years—or that those unexpected connections would open doors to the best part of the journey for me.

As already noted, my Aunt Mary (Jencyowski) MacKinnon is the only relative left in my parents' generation. She is fast approaching her 89th birthday! In an effort to gather research for this book, I was most fortunate to find her a few years ago. I now enjoy a relationship with her that I had not experienced before. Through her, I have also reunited with my MacKinnon cousins after too many absent years.

Furthermore, I have located and visited several relatives, including my cousin Dottie Dunn in New Hampshire who has since then passed; Dottie's brother Billy Dunn in Ft. Myers, FL; a distant cousin Barbara (Duff) McCarthy in Naples, FL; and Mike Duff on Cape Cod, my cousin Tommy Duff's oldest son.

Additionally, Leigh and I have made some wonderful new friends (some are relatives, some are not!) in Nova Scotia and Newfoundland, including Joselyn at the Antigonish Heritage Center, Kitty MacFarlane who still resides in the old MacKinnon home, and distant cousins Joe Byrne and Alice Finn in St. John's. What I have concluded is that we all have a deep and profound curiosity to know where we came from. With the incredible advances in technology, communication, and travel that we have experienced in the past fifty years, the world has become a much smaller place. I think it's safe to say that our ancestors would be amazed.

Unfortunately, my parents couldn't benefit from the research that's been compiled. I know they would have enjoyed learning more about those who came before them. My mother died on my birthday in 1977 at the age of 68. Subsequently, Dad married a very nice lady from Quincy, Dorothy Horgan, with whom he shared life until his passing in 1993 at 87.

Edward J. Duff, 1988.

Alice C. (McKinnon) Duff, 1973.

In reflecting on the lives of those mentioned in this book, the concept of "neighbors" has taken on a new meaning for me. Though this research began with an interest in gaining a fundamental understanding of our family origin, I hope it has stimulated a desire in others to take it to the next level. The groundwork is set: I would encourage any of my Duff/McKinnon extended (and extensive!) family with the wherewithal and the interest to pursue the dream of learning more about who you are. The same goes for any non-relatives who might happen to be reading these pages. After all, I still ponder that luncheon several years ago when I was deeply embarrassed by colleagues who were well versed in their respective family histories, but I was not! Not anymore. I now know who I am and where I came from. And I hope our ancestors would be pleased to know that generations later, we have cared enough to learn about them.

REFERENCES

Periodicals and Research Centers

Antigonish Heritage Center, Antigonish, Nova Scotia—Family trees and other records.

Archdiocese of St. John's Roman Catholic Archives. St. John's, Newfoundland.

Boston Globe, Boston Traveler, Quincy Patriot Ledger, etc.—various newspaper articles.

MacLean, Raymond A., *History of Antigonish, Volumes I and II.* Antigonish. NS: Casket Printing & Publishing Co., 1976.

Massachusetts Archives. Columbia Point Archives building files. Dorchester, MA.

National Personnel Records Center. St. Louis, MO—military records.

New York City Office of Vital Records.

New York Police Department Archives.

Ormond, Douglas Somers. *A Century Ago at Arichat and Antigonish . . .:*

Reminiscences of Mary Belle Grant Ormond. Lancelot Press, 1985.

Queen Elizabeth II Library. Genealogical Section. Memorial University of Newfoundland.

Registry of Vital Records and Statistics, Commonwealth of Massachusetts. Dorchester, MA— various birth, marriage, and death certificates.

The Rooms Provincial Archives. St. John's, Newfoundland.

St. Francis Xavier University. University Archives. Antigonish, Nova Scotia.

Seary, E.R. and Sheila M.P. Lynch. *Family Names of the Island of Newfoundland.* Montreal, Canada: McGill-Queen's University Press, 1998.

Veitch, Mary G. *Come Ashore to Holyrood: A Folk History of Holyrood.* St. John's Newfoundland: Creative Publishers, 1989.

Online Sources

Ancestry.com—various web pages.

Antigonish Diocesan History—various web pages.

Dictionary of Canadian Biography—various web pages.

FamilySearch.org—various web pages.

Newfoundland's Grand Banks. Online at ngb.chebucto.org/.

Wikipedia.org—various online encyclopedia pages.

Other

Numerous emails containing family information sent to the author by Joe Byrne, Alice Finn, and others from NL; the author distributed and discussed the emails among living Duff relatives.

Conversations with both formal and "informal" researchers and contacts.

ABOUT THE AUTHOR

WILLIAM H. DUFF attended Catholic grammar and high schools in the Boston area. At his father's urging, he continued his education at Boston College, graduating in 1970 with a bachelor's degree in accounting. In 1971, after a three-year courtship, he married Regis College graduate Leigh A. Alogna from West Haven, CT, who was teaching elementary school at the time.

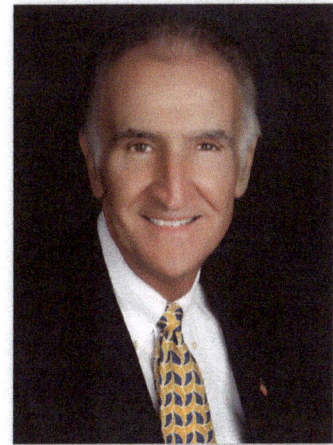

William H. Duff

After four years in the U.S. Marine Corps, Mr. Duff was appointed a Special Agent with the FBI, a position that afforded him career assignments in various parts of the country including San Francisco, Washington, D.C., and New York City. In 1981 he attained an MBA degree from Golden Gate University in San Francisco. Mrs. Duff went on to law school and pursued a legal career over the next thirty years specializing in insurance and banking law. Although retired, she holds bar memberships in Virginia, New York, and Florida.

Mr. Duff retired from the FBI in 2001. They have no children and reside in Juno Beach, FL, and Branford, CT.

INDEX

This is a person-name-only index. Birth dates may be used to identify persons of the same name. An n appended to a page number indicates a footnote. Letters A through L indicate genealogy chart locations. Underscores (_____) replace an unknown first or last name. The maiden name of a married woman is enclosed in parentheses, as is the surname of each previous husband.

A

Adam
_____ (Captain), 24
William, iv
Alogna, Leigh Adele, vii–xx, 35, 54, 122, E
Arceneaux
Delores "Dottie" (Dunn) (Marshall), D, 45–46, 121
Ernest J., 45

B

Blanford, Samuel, 24
Browning, D. M., 9, 18
Butler, James, 18

Byrne
Ellen (Wall), 12
Joe, xiv–xviii, 35, 122
John, 12
Margaret, xvii–xviii, C, 12–13, 27, 31, 32, 37
Peter, xvii

C

Cameron
Eunice (MacKinnon), 75, 77, A
Hugh, 77, A
John R., 72
Chabot, Rebecca (MacKinnon), 68
Chisholm, Jeannet, 67, 75, A

Index 133

L

LaCour
    Bridget, 23, 25, K
    Theophilus, 25
Lawley, George, 111n25
Lee
    Alice, xviii–xix, 35–37, 122
    Catherine "Kitty" (McGrath), 36, G
    Patrick, G
Locke
    Alice, 99n20
    Anne B., vi, 49, 81–83, 91, 99n20, 101, 106, 111n24, 113, B
    Charles J., 99
    Edward (b. 1854), 81, 91
    Edward L. (b. 1889), 99, 99n20
    Edward L. (b. 1972), 99n20
    Edward L., Jr. (b. 1916), 99
    Edward P. (b. 1925), 99
    Elizabeth D. "Aunt Bess," 94–98
    Evelyn, 99n20
    Evelyn F. (b. 1922), 99
    Genevieve Marie (Sister) "Aunt Molly," 69, 92–93, 94, 99n20
    Helen Agnes (Evans), 99
    Joseph, 99n20
    Marion E. (McLaughlin), 99
    Mary C. "Molly," 69, 92–93, 94
    Mary G. (Dolan), 81, 91
    Rita, 99n20
    Rita M. (b. 1918), 99
    Thomas L. "Cousin Tommy," 99
Lunny
    family, iv
    Alice Anastasia (O'Brien), 110
    James, 111
    James Joseph, 110
    Jim, vii

    John (son of John and Ruth), 111
    John Francis (b. 1910) "Uncle John," 109–111, 114, B
    Ruth (dau. of John and Ruth), 111
    Ruth Marie (McKinnon) "Aunt Ruthie" (b. 1915), 101, 108–111, B
Lyons, Alice, H

M

MacDonald
    family/clan, 58–59, 64
    Ann, 66, A
    Christina, 77–79, 81n17, B
    Laughlin, 67, B
    Mary, 66–67
    Mary (MacKinnon), 66, 67, B
    Roderick "Rory Denoon," 77–78
    Sarah, 66, A
MacEachern, *family*, 64
MacFarlane
    Andrew, 76, A
    Catherine (MacKinnon), 75, 76, A
    Colin Francis, 76
    John, 76
    Kitty (_____), ix–x, 122
    Mary, 76
    Ronald Andrew, 76–77
MacIsaac
    family, 64
    Angus "The Tailor," 76, A
    John Angus, 76
    Margaret, 68, B
    Mary (MacKinnon), 75, 76, A
    William Bernard, 76
MacKay
    John, 15
    Mary, I, 19

www.ingramcontent.com/pod-product-compliance
Lightning Source LLC
Chambersburg PA
CBHW041605260326
41914CB00012B/1393